Waterwise Plants for
Sustainable Gardens

Waterwise Plants for Sustainable Gardens

200 Drought-Tolerant Choices for All Climates

Lauren Springer Ogden

and Scott Ogden

TIMBER PRESS
Portland ✳ London

Published in 2011 by Timber Press, Inc.

The Haseltine Building
133 S.W. Second Avenue, Suite 450
Portland, Oregon 97204-3527
www.timberpress.com

2 The Quadrant
135 Salusbury Road
London NW6 6RJ
www.timberpress.co.uk

Printed in China

Library of Congress Cataloging-in-Publication Data

Ogden, Lauren Springer.
  Waterwise plants for sustainable gardens : 200 drought-
tolerant choices for all climates / Lauren Springer Ogden
and Scott Ogden. — 1st ed.
      p. cm.
  Includes bibliographical references and index.
  ISBN 978-1-60469-169-6
  1. Drought-tolerant plants—United States. 2. Xeriscap-
ing—United States. I. Ogden, Scott. II. Title.
  SB439.8.O34 2011
  635.9'525—dc22   2011012386

A catalog record for this book is also available from the
British Library.

Contents

Introduction

Rewarding Gardens Under Rainless Skies

IN THIS BOOK we have brought together two hundred beautiful plants especially selected for gardens that experience drought at some point during the year. Climate is changing and weather is becoming more erratic and unpredictable all over, even in traditionally moist regions. More and more people now grow plants in dry parts of the West, while expanding populations strain water supplies around the globe. Sustainability is the word of the day and for the future; plants that need little water and tolerate drought offer solutions for gardeners and homeowners everywhere. Plants featured here include stunning performers that are reliable under ordinary landscape conditions as well as drought. We've included many adapted widely enough to enrich gardens not only in arid western North America but also in the Northeast, Midwest, Southeast, Pacific Northwest, and United Kingdom.

Choosing the best plants is the starting point for creating a sustainable, rewarding garden, what we advocate as plant-driven design, and what we hope to help you with in this book. Intelligent gardens and landscapes are democratic. If a plant is beautiful, well adapted to the site and region, and not overly aggressive or invasive, it deserves consideration. If it needs little input in terms of soil amendment, fertilizer, or ongoing care, better yet. If it supports a range of creatures with food, cover, or nesting places, it's a win-win for all. We have used these criteria to pick the two hundred plants described here. With drought-resistant plants, less is truly more.

Gardening with Limited Water

When fully established, plants in this book all remain attractive with just 1 inch of water (rain or irrigation) every two weeks during the hottest part of peak growing season. They need much less during cooler times and when plants are not in full, active growth. For practical purposes this is how we define low-water, waterwise, or drought-tolerant plants. New plantings require more regular water: 1 inch (rain or irrigation) every week through the first growing season, trees sometimes for a second season.

In nature many plants rely on residual fall, winter, or spring moisture from snowmelt or seasonal rains; they grow strongly early in the season, then enter a resting phase during hotter, drier weather unless awakened by thundershowers or monsoonal rains. Infrequent deep irrigation encourages plants to root deeply and makes them more durable in drought. Frequent shallow irrigation can have the opposite effect and may bring alkaline salts to the surface, tying up nutrients and burning plant roots. Placing cisterns to collect rainwater, or creating curb cuts, swales, and rain gardens to redirect and conserve runoff, and building up and increasing the depth of soil over shallow rocky terrain all maximize capture, preservation, and availability of precious water.

Inorganic mulches such as pea gravel or grit in neutral colors make natural, long-lasting surfaces for waterwise gardens that help reduce soil temperatures while limiting moisture loss and the need to irrigate. Organic mulch materials such as shredded bark, wood chips, and compost are not natural to dryland environments and are best avoided near most drought-tolerant plants, as they may tie up nutrients and inhibit growth while decaying and can promote disease as well as release substances harmful to plants. Trees have deeper roots and thick protective bark and naturally grow amid fallen leaves and woody debris, so they are an exception to this.

All the plants in this book prefer well-drained soils; none require added fertilizer in garden situations.

What You'll Find Here

For each of our two hundred plant selections we've included symbols and text indicating common and botanical names, preference for sun or shade, mature size, general bloom periods (though these vary with climate and region), and where the plant is best adapted. Zones refer to the USDA zone chart on page 11; we include important additional regional information such as tolerance to heat and humidity, and performance on the West Coast (which applies to similar Mediterranean climates as well). We also let you know if a plant is native to North America, and if it's beneficial to wildlife, while not leaving out if it's resistant to browsing deer—a common concern from coast to coast.

For climates that endure both dry periods and excessive moisture, we've noted plants that tolerate brief periods of standing water. We've also added design ideas for how to place and combine each plant with other low-water plants. At the end of most plant profiles we also mention related low-water plants to give you even more choices adapted to varied climates.

We hope this distillation of our three decades of experience designing and tending gardens in zones 4 through 10 will serve you in ways that few other books can. What's more, we hope you enjoy these plants in your garden or landscape as much as we do.

Key to Symbols

	EVERGREEN
	SEMI-EVERGREEN
	DECIDUOUS
	FULL SUN (includes all-day and full-west sun)
	PART SHADE (includes dappled light, bright indirect light, and morning sun)
	FULL SHADE (no direct sun)
	TOLERATES brief periods of standing water
	rarely browsed by DEER
	attracts BEES with nectar and/or pollen
	attracts BUTTERFLIES with nectar and/or pollen
	attracts HUMMINGBIRDS with nectar and/or pollen

USDA Zones

Here are the average annual minimum temperatures for USDA zones referred to in the book:

Zone	Temperature in °F	Temperature in °C
1	below −50	−45.6 and below
2a	−45 to −50	−42.8 to −45.4
2b	−40 to −45	−40.0 to −42.7
3a	−35 to −40	−37.3 to −40.0
3b	−30 to −35	−34.5 to −37.2
4a	−25 to −30	−31.7 to −34.4
4b	−20 to −25	−28.9 to −31.6
5a	−15 to −20	−26.2 to −28.8
5b	−10 to −15	−23.4 to −26.1
6a	−5 to −10	−20.6 to −23.3
6b	0 to −5	−17.8 to −20.5
7a	5 to 0	−15.0 to −17.7
7b	10 to 5	−12.3 to −15.0
8a	15 to 10	−9.5 to −12.2
8b	20 to 15	−6.7 to −9.4
9a	25 to 20	−3.9 to −6.6
9b	30 to 25	−1.2 to −3.8
10a	35 to 30	1.6 to −1.1
10b	40 to 35	4.4 to 1.7
11	40 and above	4.5 and above

Trees

Large and long lived, trees define the skylines of gardens and landscapes, while creating rich habitats for birds and other wildlife as well as shade for people. To help in selection we've noted how quickly each tree grows and its eventual mature size.

Acer grandidentatum

bigtooth maple

grows slowly to 30–40 feet tall and 20–30 feet wide

best in zones 4–8

special attributes: Native to western North America, this under-used tree offers lush-looking lobed leaves, glowing orange autumnal foliage, and pale bark similar to sugar maple but is among the few maples with drought resistance. Also tolerates heavy and alkaline soils. Often grows multistemmed but can be trained to a single trunk. The New Mexican selection 'Manzano' is faster growing and more treelike. Bigtooth maples native to the Wasatch Mountains of Utah are especially cold hardy; those from Texas and Mexico are better for hot climates.

design ideas: Fresh-looking specimen tree. Plant in naturalistic groupings with large grasses and intermingle with evergreen trees to accentuate the beautiful fall leaf coloration.

related low-water trees: Tatarian maple (*Acer tataricum*) has slightly smaller, three-lobed leaves, and some selections bear showy persistent red-winged fruit. Fall color ranges from yellow through orange and red. Best in zones 3–7.

Calia secundiflora (formerly *Sophora secundiflora*)

Texas mountain laurel

grows slowly to 10–25 feet tall and half as wide

best in zones 8–10 with hot summers and alkaline soils

special attributes: This multistemmed southwestern native hoists craggy stems with profuse, glossy pinnate foliage; it grows lush and dense even in desert heat and glaring sun. Thrives in warm coastal conditions. Wisteria-like blossoms in early spring smell like grape soda and attract bees. Woody pods enclose bright red poisonous beans when ripe. In late summer satiny tassel-like buds form for next year's flowers. Feeds caterpillars of indigo, blue, and orange sulphur butterflies.

design ideas: Combine with the foliages of silvery ceniza and germander, feathery bird of paradise and acacia, spiky agave and sotol. Blossoms coincide nicely with Lady Banks' rose, *Yucca treculeana*, and Texas redbud.

related low-water trees: *Calia secundiflora* 'Silver Peso' has gray foliage and dark violet flowers, is less humidity tolerant.

Cedrus deodara

deodar cedar

grows quickly to 50–80 feet tall and 25–40 feet wide

best in zones 7–10, 'Kashmir' and 'Shalimar' hardy to zone 6

special attributes: Deodar cedar is a graceful conifer with a nodding, conical silhouette and drooping branches with soft gray-green needles draping down to the ground. Mature trees bear upright purplish cones. This Himalayan native's name, *deodar*, means "tree of the gods" in Sanskrit.

design ideas: Grow singly as a stately specimen or create a forestlike grove. Use as a soft screen or lacy frame for landscape views.

related low-water trees: Other large, soft-textured, deer-resistant evergreen trees incude western North American native incense cedar (*Calocedrus decurrens*) and oriental arborvitae (*Platycladus orientalis*), both with flattened sprays of foliage and hardy into zone 5b.

Cercis canadensis var. *texensis*

Texas redbud

grows quickly to 15–25 feet tall and wide

best in zones 7–9, worth trying in zone 6 in the West

special attributes: Native to Texas, Oklahoma, and northeastern Mexico, this small tree is loved for its deep pink spring blossoms clustered on bare branches. Attracts bees. Kidney-shaped leaves are glossy, more sun tolerant and less heart shaped than typical redbud foliage, and turn golden yellow in fall. Flattened seedpods are wine colored before ripening. Named selections such as 'Oklahoma' (magenta flowered), 'White Texas' (white flowered), 'Merlot' (purple leaves), and 'Traveller' (weeping) are usually grafted on eastern redbud rootstock and therefore need deeper soil and regular watering. Cotton root rot limits use in some areas. Feeds caterpillars of the Io moth.

design ideas: Combine with Texas mountain laurel and white-flowered Lady Banks' rose. Underplant with a carpet of grape hyacinths.

related low-water trees: Mexican redbud (*Cercis canadensis* var. *mexicana*) has a finer texture and is shrubbier. Western redbud (*C. occidentalis*) is better farther west. Judas tree (*C. siliquastrum*) is a larger, leafier tree from the Middle East.

Chilopsis linearis

desert willow

grows quickly to 15–25 feet tall and wide

best in zones 7–10 with hot summers, worth trying in sheltered positions in zones 5b–6 in the West

special attributes: A fine-textured southwestern native, desert willow has slender spreading branches and willowlike foliage. Endures saline soils. Casts filtered shade. Generous trusses of large pink, burgundy, white, or bicolored snapdragon-like blossoms open from summer to frost; white-flowered forms are noticeably fragrant. Bees, bumblebees, and hummingbirds all frequent the flowers. Beanlike pods ripen in late summer and fall; the selections Timeless Beauty and 'Art's Seedless' are nearly fruitless.

design ideas: Silhouette against masonry walls. Combine with larger cacti, agaves, grasses, and long-blooming companions such as Mexicali penstemon, salvias, red yucca, and ceniza. Good patio tree.

related low-water trees: ×*Chitalpa tashkentensis* 'Pink Dawn' is a slightly larger and coarser hybrid between desert willow and catalpa with light pink blossoms.

Corylus colurna

Turkish filbert

grows slowly to 30–40 feet tall and 15–20 feet wide

best in zones 4–7, also zones 8–9 on the West Coast

special attributes: This handsome upright, teardrop-shaped tree has dense leathery rich green foliage, making a bushy silhouette. Strong wood and branching habit make the tree resistant to wind or snow break-age. Pale bark is pretty in winter. Basically maintenance free except for leaf raking where needed.

design ideas: Ideal street tree or for narrow spaces near buildings. Can lend a formal look, would work nicely as a tough, good-looking, easy-care, long-lived allee planting.

Crataegus ambigua

Russian hawthorn

grows moderately to 15–25 feet tall and 20–25 feet wide

best in zones 3–7, resents humid heat

special attributes: More drought tolerant than most other hawthorns, this one is a rounded, full tree with fine texture. Snowy masses of small flowers in late spring for two to three weeks attract bees. Their scent is less offensive than that of most hawthorn blossoms. Cherrylike clustered fruit persists into fall, feeding birds. Small toothed, lobed foliage turns amber before falling. Branch growth is irregular and curvaceous, with peeling bark, lending a sense of age and grace while still young; beautiful as a multistemmed tree. Spines are much fewer and less vicious than on other hawthorns.

design ideas: Plant several trees as a naturalistic grove or a single one as an accent. Ideal with underplantings of shade-tolerant perennials and ground covers thanks to its benevolent roots. Plant ivory or blue sedge and grape hyacinths beneath.

Cupressus arizonica

Arizona cypress

grows quickly to 15–35 feet tall and half as wide

best in zones 7–10, hardiest forms to zones 5 and 6

special attributes: A silvery southwestern native, Arizona cypress has aromatic scalelike foliage in sprays and a pyramidal habit. Mature trees make furrowed bark and bear small rounded cones. 'Cookes Peak' strain is the hardiest, to zone 5.

design ideas: Use as a specimen, hedge, screen, or windbreak. Beautiful blue-gray foil for red-orange fall foliage of sumac, Spanish oak, bigtooth maple.

related low-water trees: Smooth Arizona cypress (*Cupressus glabra*) has reddish, peeling bark. 'Blue Ice', 'Gareei' are upright selections; 'Silver Smoke', 'Carolina Sapphire' grow wider. Western native Modoc cypress (*C. bakeri*) has olive green foliage. Southwestern native alligator juniper (*Juniperus deppeana*), not tolerant of humid heat, is

more open, with checkered bark. All are hardy in zones 6–10. Selections of Rocky Mountain juniper (*J. scopulorum*) are gray, green, or blue and denser in habit, female plants bear small blue fruits, hardy to zone 3, resent humid heat.

Forestiera pubescens subsp. *neomexicana*

New Mexican olive

grows quickly to 10–15 feet tall and 8–12 feet wide

best in zones 4–10

special attributes: This multistemmed western North American native bears tiny, very early flowers that envelop the plant in a soft yellow, bee-filled haze, followed by small lime green foliage. Also attracts butterflies. Pale cream-colored bark is worth uncovering by pruning out lower branchlets. Female plants set loads of fruit that resembles small blueberries; birds love these. Luminescent yellow fall foliage. A fresh green, fine-textured small tree that lights up muted greens and grays common to drought-tolerant plantings. May self-sow.

design ideas: Integrate with junipers, pines, or cypresses for a naturalistic planting of varied colors and textures. A nice accent tree by a wall or a house corner when the branches are limbed up, offering good cooling shade for building walls in summer. Combine with large blue agaves, yuccas, and sotols.

related low-water trees: Olive (*Olea europaea*) makes an evergreen tree to 25 feet tall and wide, with gray-green foliage and a gnarled, picturesque habit. Fruitless and dwarf forms are available. Best in zones 9–10 with low humidity, hardier forms such as 'Arbequina' to zone 8.

Juniperus virginiana 'Taylor'

'Taylor' columnar juniper

grows moderately to 20–30 feet tall and 4–5 feet wide

best in zones 4–10

special attributes: A classic columnar evergreen for colder regions, this narrow selection of a North American native gives a distinctively elegant, dark gray-green silhouette. Less prone to splaying in snow than other upright junipers. Extremely tight branches and foliage sprays give an almost sheared look. Feeds caterpillars of several hairstreak butterfly species.

design ideas: Ideal for narrow spaces, as a tidy, easy-care evergreen screen, for formal or Mediterranean-inspired gardens, or as an exciting accent in a wilder, less geometric garden.

related low-water trees: The most common columnar form of Italian cypress (*Cupressus sempervirens* 'Glauca') is an iconic Mediterranean tree with a narrow, vertical, almost black-green exclamation-point silhouette. It is very drought resistant once established and grows more tightly, healthily, and beautifully in lower humidity. Hardy in zones 7–10.

Pinus bungeana

lacebark pine

grows slowly to 30 or more feet tall and 20 feet wide

best in zones 4b–7, also zones 8–9 on the West Coast

special attributes: This open and airy pine offers bright green needles and beautiful bark mottled pale gray, olive green, and rust in puzzlelike shapes. Less somber looking and bulky in the landscape than most pines. Benevolent root system allows for diverse underplanting.

design ideas: Elegant as a focal point yet natural looking enough to blend into a mixed planting of trees. A background of dark evergreens or a wall of any color shows off the extraordinary bark hues and patterns best.

related low-water trees: Tanyosho pine (*Pinus densiflora* 'Umbraculifera') is smaller, typically 15–20 feet tall, with several orange-brown trunks, a dense mushroomlike head of branches, and bright green needles; best in zones 4–7, also zone 8 on the West Coast. Italian stone pine (*P. pinea*) has a similar cloudlike head but is less often multi-stemmed and eventually grows much larger; hardy in zones 7–10 with low humidity.

Pinus flexilis

limber pine

grows slowly to 30–40 feet tall and 20–30 feet wide

best in zones 3–7, also zones 8–9 on the West Coast

special attributes: This Rocky Mountain native has an irregular, picturesque growth habit. Needles are handsomely twisted and with a blue cast, giving a windswept look. Smooth pale gray bark. Tolerant of heavy and alkaline soils. 'Vanderwolf's Pyramid' is faster growing and more upright, with less character. Appealing narrow, weeping, and compact forms of limber pine are also in the trade.

design ideas: Makes a nice naturalistic specimen or informal screen. Beautiful with the red and orange fall color of sumac and bigtooth maple.

related low-water trees: Southwestern white pine, *Pinus strobiformis*, is very similar but slightly taller and faster growing than limber pine, with a more regular habit and longer, softer, paler needles. It is only slightly less hardy, zones 5–7.

Prosopis glandulosa

honey mesquite

grows slowly to 25 feet tall and 50 feet wide

best in zones 6b–10

special attributes: Honey mesquite is a graceful southwestern native with furrowed bark and drooping bright green feathery foliage. Gives a fresh look and creates filtered shade. Endures windy coastal sites. Creamy honey-scented flower spikes appear in summer, favored by bees. Seed-grown trees bear paired thorns on twigs; 'Maverick' is thornless. Feeds caterpillars of several species of blue butterflies.

design ideas: Plant as counterpoint to dark green Italian cypress or silver Mediterranean fan palm and cenizas, architectural agaves and sotols. Thornless form makes a fine patio tree and provides diffuse summer shading against south- or west-facing building walls.

related low-water trees: Southwestern native sweet acacia (*Acacia farnesiana*) carries fragrant golden orange blossoms in late winter and early spring. Thornless palo verde (*Parkinsonia* 'Desert Museum') opens small yellow blooms from spring to fall in flushes. Both make feathery broad-spreading trees hardy to zone 8.

Prunus armeniaca

apricot

grows moderately to 15–25 feet tall and wide

best in zones 5–10, 'Chinese' and 'Mormon' to zone 4

special attributes: This is a small tree with very early delicate pink flowers, attractive to bees. Cultivated for sweet fruits and sometimes for edible kernels. Heart-shaped leaves emerge reddish, remain fresh green through summer, and turn amber, orange, or red in fall. Soft yellow- or white-fleshed fruits may not mature dependably every year; choose locally recommended varieties for best production. Most are self-fruitful; 'Moongold' and 'Sungold' pollinate each other. Site trees on north- or east-facing exposures to protect flowers and fruit set from late frosts.

design ideas: Plant near evergreen backdrop to show off pale flowers. Underplant with stompable sedge for fruit drop and harvest.

related low-water trees: 'Josephine', a nonfruiting hybrid flowering apricot, opens large pink flowers in late winter; 'Hall's Hardy' almond (*Prunus dulcis*) makes a small rounded tree with pale pink flowers in early spring, shiny foliage, and edible nuts; both are best in zones 6–9.

Ptelea trifoliata

hop tree, wafer ash

grows moderately to 15–20 feet tall and wide

best in zones 3–10

special attributes: Native from the Northeast to the Southwest, this adaptable small vase-shaped tree grows multistemmed. Clusters of tiny green flowers in early summer have a sweet, permeating fragrance and attract bees of many species. Female trees produce showy papery clusters of chartreuse fruits. Shiny fresh green leaflets, golden in the selection 'Aurea', grow in threes and turn a luminescent yellow in fall. May self-sow. Feeds caterpillars of several swallowtail butterfly species.

design ideas: Because it is one of the most lush-looking woody plants for dry places, the unassuming hop tree deserves a place amid large shrubs or beneath larger trees. Also nice on a patio or to shade south-facing windows, casting dappled shade and lending an oasis feel.

Quercus buckleyi

Spanish oak, Texas red oak

grows moderately to 35–45 feet tall and 25–35 feet wide

best in zones 5b–8

special attributes: A southwestern native, this oak has single or multiple trunks and spreading branches. Sharply lobed foliage remains shining green through summer heat; turns russet, maroon, and scarlet in late fall and stays colorful for weeks. Oak wilt and cotton root rot limit use in some areas. Feeds caterpillars of several skipper and hairstreak butterfly species, as well as admirals. Nuttall's oak (*Quercus texana*) and Shumard oak (*Quercus shumardii*) are often confused with *Q. buckleyi* but do not tolerate prolonged drought or strong alkalinity.

design ideas: Treasured shade tree or specimen. Fall color especially effective mingled with pines, junipers, and Arizona cypress.

related low-water trees: Chisos red oak (*Quercus gravesii*) has pendant leaves turning amber to red in December; Canby oak (*Q. canbyi*) is nearly evergreen and hardy in zones 7–9.

Quercus macrocarpa

bur oak

grows moderately to 35–60 feet tall and wide, or up to twice that under ideal conditions

best in zones 3–9

special attributes: This lofty prairie native is admired for its rugged beauty and longevity. Oversized acorns in curious burlike cups inspire the common name. Large, coarsely lobed leaves are dark green above, pale beneath, turn yellow in autumn. Imposing branches covered in fissured bark cast welcome shade; trees achieve large size on deep soils.

design ideas: Site west of buildings to give cooling summer shade. Underplant with sedges, spring-blooming Grecian windflowers, creeping grapeholly.

related low-water trees: Colorado foothills oak (*Quercus ×mazei*), zones 4–8, is a smaller natural hybrid of bur oak and Gambel oak. Midsize Lacey oak (*Q. laceyi*), zones 5b–8, has wavy bluish leaves. Large chinquapin oak (*Q. muhlenbergii*), zones 4–8, has serrated leaves that are silvery below. Leaves of all three turn red to amber in fall.

Styphnolobium japonicum (formerly *Sophora japonica*)

pagoda tree, scholar tree

grows moderately to 30–50 feet tall and wide

best in zones 4–8, also zones 9–10 on the West Coast, needs hot summers

special attributes: This is a fine-textured tree with a rounded crown. Lustrous pinnate leaves give lush appearance, cast filtered shade. Cream flowers appear in branched spikes in mid to late summer on mature trees, attracting bees. Tolerates pollution. 'Regent' and 'Princeton Upright' are fast-growing, compact selections; 'Pendula' is weeping, nonflowering.

design ideas: Choice street tree, courtyard specimen.

related low-water trees: Eve's necklace (*Styphnolobium affine*), native to Texas and neighboring states, zones 7–9, makes a shrubby tree 15–20 feet tall with shining green foliage and modest pink to cream flowers in late spring.

Ungnadia speciosa

Mexican buckeye

grows moderately to 10–20 feet tall and half as wide

best in zones 7–10 with hot summers, worth trying in zone 6 in the West

special attributes: This multistemmed southwestern native has ashlike divided leaves that turn clear yellow in fall. Small pink to wine-colored flowers line twigs profusely in spring and attract bees. Interesting three-lobed woody pods enclose marble-sized seeds, decorate winter branches.

design ideas: Place at top of berm, wall, or embankment to show off flowers. Combine with grape hyacinths. Good understory tree.

related low-water trees: Yellowhorn (*Xanthoceras sorbifolium*) is a small multistemmed tree hardy in zones 5b–9 that opens showy clusters of fragrant white flowers in midspring amid shiny green foliage.

Shrubs and Subshrubs

Shrubs and subshrubs create a visual framework that lasts
all year. They bring a sense of continuity as well as changing
aspects to celebrate the seasons. The term subshrub applies
to smaller, soft-wooded, twiggy bushes typical of dry climates.
Although these usually retain a woody framework, you can cut
them back partially to limit their size and make them bushier.
In cold climates some subshrubs may need to be treated as
nonwoody perennials.

Abelia ×grandiflora

glossy abelia

grows 4 feet tall and 6 feet wide

best in zones 6–10

special attributes: A free-flowering, adaptable heirloom, glossy abelia has a relaxed form and a fine texture. Spraylike branches bear pointed, glossy leaves that turn bronze in winter. White tubular flowers appear throughout summer, attracting butterflies, bees, and hummingbirds. Pink calyces hang on after blossoms drop, extending color. Selections with dwarf habits, pink flowers, gold or white variegated foliage are available.

design ideas: Abelias stay full to the ground, making good hedges or specimens on top of raised walls and berms. Combine with aromatic aster, 'Grey Owl' juniper, 'Powis Castle' artemisia, or smokebush.

related low-water shrubs: *Abelia chinensis* and *A. mosanensis* are deciduous shrubs with clusters of fragrant white flowers attractive to butterflies. Hybrids of *A. chinensis* such as 'Rose Creek' and 'Ruby Anniversary' combine semi-evergreen foliage with clusters of scented white blossoms.

Amorpha canescens

leadplant

grows 2–3 feet tall and 3–4 feet wide

best in zones 3–7

special attributes: This North American prairie native has a billowing form and fine-textured gray-green pinnate foliage. Indigo flower spikes dusted with orange pollen, attractive to bees and butterflies, top the branches in midsummer. Often newer growth dies back in dry or severely cold winters; cut back to live wood in spring to keep neater. Very late to begin growth in spring. Feeds caterpillars of the dogface butterfly.

design ideas: The fine gray foliage combines nicely with evergreen blue desert grapeholly. For an ethereal silver shrub planting, mingle with artemisia, lavender, santolina, rabbitbrush, ephedra, and Russian sage. Nice with midsize bunchgrasses such as little bluestem or alkali sacaton to evoke its native haunts, or paired with summer-blooming prairie natives such as gaillardia, sundrop, winecup, and butterfly weed.

Artemisia 'Powis Castle'

hybrid wormwood

grows 2 feet high and 3 feet wide

best in zones 6–10, herbaceous perennial in zone 5 in the West

special attributes: A mounding subshrub that remains handsome all year, 'Powis Castle' wormwood is treasured for its dense habit and finely divided silver-felted leaves. This nonflowering hybrid is more tolerant of heat and humidity, and longer lived than other artemisias. Shear to maintain dense rounded form or allow to drape and sprawl.

design ideas: The shimmering foliage enhances evening gardens alongside datura, crinum lilies, and evening primrose. Leaves combine well with flowers or colored foliage. Sprawling habit is nice for softening edges and draping over slopes.

related low-water shrubs: For colder climates (zones 4–8), *Artemisia absinthium* 'Lambrook Silver' is more compact, and seafoam sage (*A. versicolor*) forms a silvery, lichen-like mat less than a foot tall and twice as wide. More humidity tolerant but less hardy, *Artemisia* 'Huntington' (zones 7–9) is more compact and paler silver than 'Powis Castle'.

Bauhinia lunarioides

Chihuahuan orchid tree, *pata de vaca*

grows 15 feet tall and wide

best in zones 8–10 in the West with hot summers, worth trying in hot, dry sites in the Southeast

special attributes: This large multistemmed southwestern native shrub features unique butterfly-shaped gray-green foliage. Clusters of small fragrant white or pink orchidlike blossoms appear in spring and after fall rains, attracting bees and butterflies. Often self-sows. Feeds caterpillars of the long-tailed skipper butterfly.

design ideas: Plant near paths, entrance gates, and walls to enjoy unusual leaves, fragrant flowers, and visiting butterflies.

related low-water shrubs: *Bauhinia macranthera* and *B. ramosissima* have upward-facing pink flowers. *Bauhinia bartlettii* has lavender blossoms, and white *B. mexicana* is everblooming. All are small, shrubby orchid trees from northeastern Mexico.

Caesalpinia gilliesii

bird of paradise shrub, paradise poinciana

grows 6–12 feet tall and half as wide

best in zones 7–10 with hot summers, worth trying in zone 6 in the West

special attributes: This vase-shaped shrub has lacy, intricate gray-green foliage and flamboyant clusters of yellow flowers with long red stamens that create an exotic look. Blossoms appear late spring through summer, attracting bees, butterflies, and humming-birds. Self-sows mildly.

design ideas: Plant near sunny walls or with silver or gray-leafed companion plants.

related low-water shrubs: Barbados pride (*Caesalpinia pulcherrima*), zones 8–10, is a thorny, heat-loving shrub that succeeds as a nonwoody perennial in protected parts of zone 7b in the West. It combines feathery green leaves with large trusses of brilliant gold-to-orange flowers.

Caryopteris ×clandonensis

blue mist spirea

grows 3–4 feet tall and wide

best in zones 5–8, also zones 9–10 on the West Coast

special attributes: A rounded, twiggy shrub with narrow gray-green foliage, blue mist spirea bears masses of clustered small blue flowers for many weeks in late summer, a most welcome time. Dried seed capsules remain attractive into winter but self-seeding may become a nuisance. Bees and bumblebees throng to the flowers. Cut shrub back by a quarter or a third in early spring to keep compact and vigorous. Golden-leafed forms are not as drought resistant.

design ideas: Looks good with almost anything and has become overused in uninspired ways. Always welcome amid late-summer-blooming perennials such as agastaches, datura, and prairie gayfeather; in the dry shrub border with autumn sage, artemisia, rabbitbrush, and Apache plume; or with beefy grasses such as big bluestem, various muhlies, Atlas fescue, and Indian grass.

43

Chaenomeles hybrids

flowering quince

grows 2–10 feet tall and 3–10 feet wide

best in zones 5–9

special attributes: This group includes rounded heirloom shrubs *Chaenomeles japonica* (shorter and wider spreading) and *C. speciosa* (taller and more upright), and hybrids of the two, beloved for beautiful early, bee-visited flowers before leaves appear. Blossoms look like small 1- to 2-inch roses in coral, orange, or red, with white, peach, and pink selections as well. The shrub is impenetrably twiggy and slightly thorny, with modest yet glossy green foliage that emerges reddish. Excellent for cutting and forcing. May show leaf yellowing in hot desert climates.

design ideas: Use as a barrier hedge or background plant, best placed for backlighting by low morning or afternoon sun when in bloom in early spring, or with a dark evergreen background to show off the flowers.

Cotinus coggygria

smoke bush

grows 8–25 feet tall and 8–15 feet wide

best in zones 5–8, also zones 9–10 on the West Coast

special attributes: Smoke bush bears billowing smokelike panicles of tiny flowers that start off rosy, attracting myriad bees, and turn bronze and then buff over several weeks in summer. Foliage is blue-green, burgundy, or golden in selections, sometimes with gold or orange fall color. May suffer dieback during severe winters but tolerates harsh pruning, responding with vigorous new growth. Self-sows mildly.

design ideas: The foliage and flower plumes deserve backlighting or placement against a wall. Smoke bush tucks nicely between other large shrubs and small trees such as desert willow, lilac, hop tree, or cutleaf sumac.

related low-water shrubs: American smoke tree (*Cotinus obovatus*), zones 4–8, has larger blue-green leaves that turn phenomenal orange, red, and burgundy in autumn. Hybrid 'Grace' has huge pink flower billows and good fall color.

Ephedra equisetina

blue joint fir

grows 3–4 feet tall, 5–6 feet wide

best in zones 5–7, also zones 8–9 on the West Coast

special attributes: The upright powder blue leafless stems of this unique plant give an unusual effect year-round, especially in winter. Female plants have red ½-inch fruit in summer and autumn following insignificant spring flowers. Spreads slowly at the base by suckers.

design ideas: Great as an accent against walls and modern architecture, or mixed with structural plants such as yuccas and agaves. Also a nice textural contrast among shrubs of all sorts. Plant wine cup or evening primrose at its base.

Ericameria nauseosa (formerly *Chrysothamnus nauseosus*)

rabbitbrush, chamisa

grows 1–6 feet tall and 2–6 feet wide

best in zones 3–8 in the West

special attributes: This intricately branched, aromatic native shrub is common on alkaline soils of the intermountain West. Its dense habit creates an irregular cloudlike form. Twigs carry wispy green or blue-gray foliage. Clusters of gold flowers appear at branch tips in fall, drawing bees and butterflies. Straw-toned seedheads and silvery or bright green twigs remain attractive through winter. Self-sows abundantly. Hard pruning in late winter encourages denser branching. Nurseries offer dwarf blue (var. *nauseosa*), tall green (var. *graveolens*) and tall blue (var. *albicaulis*) strains. Feeds caterpillars of the painted lady butterfly.

design ideas: Makes a handsome silhouette near masonry walls. Compact forms are a good choice for narrow beds adjacent to paving. Lovely in chaparral-inspired plantings with Apache plume, yuccas, and blueleaf grapeholly.

Fallugia paradoxa

Apache plume

grows 4–5 feet tall and wide

best in zones 4–9 with hot summers and low humidity

special attributes: A fine-textured southwestern native, Apache plume has pale, chalky twigs and tiny cleft foliage. White five-petaled flowers bloom profusely in late spring and intermittently all summer into fall, attracting bees and butterflies. As they ripen, fluffy pink and then white seed heads form. Prune from time to time to keep from getting straggly.

design ideas: Offers a nice textural contrast to linear yuccas and bold cacti as well as to strong architecture. Lovely when seed heads are backlit, along with interplanted grasses. Not for the more manicured garden, with its wild and woolly seed heads and casual growth habit.

Genista lydia

Lydian broom

grows 1–2 feet tall and 4–6 feet wide

best in zones 4–8

special attributes: Bright yellow pea blossoms smother this dwarf shrub in spring, attracting bees. Masses of slender sage-green stems held in a low mound make this broom appear tidy and fresh all year.

design ideas: Drape informally over rocks or plant in masses as a ground cover. Give southern exposure to encourage early bloom. Combine with dwarf bearded iris, sedums, and woolly veronica. Good on roof gardens.

related low-water shrubs: Spanish broom (*Spartium junceum*), zones 6–10, may be invasive on the West Coast but not so in desert regions. Creates a sparse upright bush with fragrant golden pea blossoms in spring. *Cytisus purgans*, hardy Spanish broom, is adapted to the same colder climates as Lydian broom and makes a larger, rounded, dense shrub with golden spring bloom and bright green stems year-round.

Jasminum nudiflorum

winter jasmine

grows 3 feet tall and wide spreading

best in zones 6–8

special attributes: Winter jasmine is a mounding shrub with slender cascading branches that bear lustrous three-part leaves in summer. Unscented, showy, tubular yellow blossoms dot the naked twigs, attracting bees for many weeks in late winter.

design ideas: Place near a south-facing wall to encourage early bloom, on an embankment or on top of a wall to show off its cascading habit. Draping stems can be allowed to layer and colonize ground as well as roof gardens.

related low-water shrubs: Showy jasmine (*Jasminum floridum*), zones 7b–10, has alternate evergreen leaves, unlike most jasmines, and bears yellow flowers in early summer. Primrose jasmine (*J. mesnyi*), zones 8–10, has larger pale evergreen foliage on taller, rampant stems, carries double light yellow blossoms in late winter.

Juniperus communis var. *saxatilis*

mountain juniper

grows 1 foot tall and 5 feet wide

best in zones 3–7, also zones 8–10 on the West Coast

special attributes: A spreading shrub native to the mountains and boreal forests of North America and Eurasia, mountain juniper has sprays of green needlelike foliage marked silver on the undersides that appear more pinelike than the foliage of other junipers. Small dark blue fruits on female plants attract wildlife. Western selections such as 'Ami-Dak' (sold as Blueberry Delight) are better for drought and heat tolerance. Thrives in dry shade as well as sun.

design ideas: This informal evergreen looks good near boulders, on slopes, under trees. Combine with creeping grapeholly and ivory sedge in dry shade. Good on roof gardens.

related low-water shrubs: Shore juniper (*Juniperus conferta* 'Blue Pacific'), zones 6–9, resembles mountain juniper but with a low habit and bluer foliage; popular ground cover best in sun.

Juniperus 'Grey Owl'

'Grey Owl' spreading juniper

grows 2–3 feet tall and 5–6 feet wide

best in zones 2–8, also zones 9–10 on the West Coast

special attributes: Loads of small pale blue fruit add to the year-round appeal of this feathery gray-green shrub. Probably a hybrid between Chinese juniper and North American native eastern red cedar, showing extreme adaptability and disease resistance in most climates.

design ideas: Junipers are much maligned due to their overuse and careless placement in so many North American landscapes over the years. 'Grey Owl' deserves a second look. It offers a low-growing, wide-spreading form excellent for fronting a shrub planting or backing low perennials and ground covers. Its foliage sprays have a lively, natural look yet are not unruly. Especially nice with plants that show red or orange fall color, and with bearded iris and small tufted grasses.

Kolkwitzia amabilis

beauty bush

grows 10–15 feet tall and wide

best in zones 4–8

special attributes: This tough heirloom shrub deserves revival. Fine-textured foliage is neatly arranged along arching branches and pale bark peels in attractive shreds on thicker stems. In early summer, the shrub covers itself in small baby-pink flowers for several weeks, attracting butterflies and bees. Golden and variegated foliage forms are available. Some pruning of the weakest and oldest branches every few years keeps it kempt.

design ideas: Handsome large shrub for background or hedging, mixed with other large shrubs such as cutleaf sumac, lilac, flowering quince. Especially nice with purple-leaf smoke bush.

Lavandula angustifolia

English lavender

grows 1–2 feet tall and 2–3 feet wide

best in zones 5–10, resents humid heat

special attributes: This aromatic herb has dense gray or green foliage and upright spikes of small violet flowers attractive to bees. Strongly fragrant blossoms and leaves. Compact varieties and selections with pink or white flowers are available.

design ideas: Place along paths for fragrance, use as edging for herb gardens; shear as formal feature or row crop in larger gardens. Combine with evening primrose, butterfly weed, striped iris, and midsize grasses such as feather grass, Atlas fescue, or silver spike grass.

related low-water shrubs: Lavandin (*Lavandula ×intermedia*) carries more slender flower spikes and is less hardy, to zone 6. 'Grosso White' has white flowers. Spanish lavender (*L. stoechas*), French lavender (*L. dentata*), *L. ×allardii*, and 'Goodwin Creek Grey' are hardy in zones 8–10. Fern leaf lavender (*L. multifida*) is frost tender, everblooming.

Leucophyllum frutescens

ceniza, Texas purple sage, barometer bush

grows 4–6 feet tall and 3–5 feet wide

best in zones 7b–10 with hot summers and alkaline soils

special attributes: Ceniza is a southwestern shrub with felted gray, green, or silver rounded foliage. Snapdragon-like flowers smother branches after thunderstorms and attract bees and hummingbirds. Selections include compact forms, and flowers in pink, lavender, purple, or white. Good in warm coastal conditions. Feeds caterpillars of checkerspot butterfly.

design ideas: Shear for denser foliage and compact habit. Spent flowers fall to decorate paving, gravel mulch. Lovely with bold agaves and large cacti. Contrast with rosemary and Texas mountain laurel.

related low-water shrubs: Slightly hardier *Leucophyllum minus* bears small silver leaves, purple flowers. *Leucophyllum langmaniae*, with lilac flowers and fresh green foliage, tolerates part shade; 'Lynn's Legacy' is everblooming. Similar *L. laevigatum* has open habit, requires sun. *Leucophyllum zygophyllum* bears violet blossoms among boxy silver leaves. All these thrive in hot interior climates but fare poorly in warm coastal regions.

Mahonia fremontii

blueleaf desert holly

grows 4–6 feet tall and wide

best in zones 4–8, also zones 9–10 on the West Coast, resents humid heat

special attributes: This western native shrub with small hollylike blue-to-lavender foliage and early honey-scented yellow flowers in dangling clusters is loved by bees. Blossoms ripen to showy ¼-inch red fruits by midsummer, savored by wildlife. May suffer leaf browning in windy, cold winters, but quick to releaf in spring. New foliage is reddish. Gardening around this plant can be miserable due to the prickly dropped leaves.

design ideas: Best in untended spots with other low-care shrubs, succulents, cacti, agaves, and yuccas because of the prickly foliage. Worth planting for its four seasons of beauty.

related low-water shrubs: Red-fruited desert holly (*Mahonia haematocarpa*) is a closely related larger shrub and often not quite as blue in leaf color. Agarita (*M. trifoliolata*) is better for very hot climates and can tolerate more humidity.

Perovskia ×hybrida

Russian sage

grows 3–5 feet tall and 4–5 feet wide

best in zones 5–10 with hot summers

special attributes: Fine-textured white stems and small, aromatic, often deeply cleft gray-green foliage make a twiggy mass topped with airy, branched spikes of lavender-blue flowers from mid to late summer well into fall. Usually dies back quite a bit in winter, and even if not, best to cut back to a foot or less in early spring to keep strong growing and compact. Attracts bees and bumblebees. Some clones spread by underground runners to form colonies while others remain solitary.

design ideas: Looks good with almost anything. Especially nice with grasses, yuccas, and agaves. Makes a superb main player amid other drought-resistant perennials and annuals in a more cottage-y floral composition.

Philadelphus lewisii 'Cheyenne'

western mock orange

grows 6–9 feet tall and wide

best in zones 3–8, also zones 9–10 on the West Coast

special attributes: This western North American native is more dense growing, wide spreading, and drought resistant than the common mock orange yet offers masses of the same beautiful, sweet-scented, four-petaled white blossoms for a few weeks in early summer, attracting bees and butterflies. Foliage is neat, arranged opposite along the stems.

design ideas: Plant close to paths, windows, or entryways to enjoy the fragrant blossoms. The white flowers are especially effective against a darker backdrop such as purple-leaf smoke bush or pine, and with a silver footing of 'Powis Castle' artemisia. Ideal for evening gardens.

related low-water shrubs: Southwestern native little-leaf mock orange (*Philadelphus microphyllus*), zones 5–9, is half the size, with tiny, almost boxwoodlike foliage and small, starry, fragrant white flowers. It is even more drought resistant than 'Cheyenne'.

Phlomis fruticosa

Jerusalem sage

grows 3 feet tall and wide

best in zones 7–10, worth trying in zone 6 in the West

special attributes: Showy whorls of golden blossoms top the branches of this sub-shrub in spring, attracting bees. The dense, rounded form and felted oblong leaves with yellowish gray undersides look handsome all year. Grows actively during cool spring or fall weather; difficult to establish in summer heat. In late fall, cuttings root so easily that they can be stuck directly into the garden.

design ideas: Combine with rosemary, santolina, lavender, and silver germander to create a Mediterranean or chaparral-inspired planting. Combine with bold leaves of agaves, yuccas, and shrub palms.

related low-water shrubs: Shorter, paler, more finely textured Cretan sage (*Phlomis cretica*), dwarf gold-leaf phlomis (*P. lanata*), low-growing large-leaf phlomis (*P.* 'Edward Bowles'), puckered gray-green Turkish phlomis (*P. bourgaei*), gold leaf phlomis (*P. aurea*), and pink phlomis (*P. italica*) are other low-water species.

Pinus nigra 'Helga'

dwarf Austrian pine

grows 4–6 feet tall and wide

best in zones 4–7, also zones 8–9 on the West Coast

special attributes: One of the toughest and most handsome compact conifers, dwarf Austrian pine is dense, rounded, and rich green with pale, resinous buds. Its strong year-round presence anchors deciduous plants. 'Hornibrookiana' is another similarly dwarf selection.

design ideas: Looks good as an accent specimen or as a team player in a shrub planting, or in a naturalistic garden amid boulders and larger rock-garden-style plants.

related low-water shrubs: Compact selections of Bosnian pine (*Pinus heldreichii* var. *leucodermis*), zones 5–6, are similar in look and in drought resistance but more prone to windburn and less heat tolerant. Dwarf Japanese red pine (*Pinus densiflora* 'Low Glow') is shorter and more flat topped, with paler green, softer needles.

Punica granatum 'Nana', also known as 'Spanish Ruby'

dwarf pomegranate

grows 3–6 feet tall and 3–4 feet wide

best in zones 7b–10 with hot summers

special attributes: This rugged shrub is native to Persia and has been cultivated there since ancient times. Showy carnation-like double orange flowers appear in summer and attract bees. Prolific miniature red-skinned fruits enclosing tart berries ripen in fall and provide juice rich in vitamins and antioxidants. Fine-textured shiny green oval foliage turns clear yellow in autumn; drab winter appearance except for persistent fruits. For fruit production, the standard nondwarf species and its selections are best, but the dwarf plant is more ornamental.

design ideas: Classic choice for a patio specimen near a sunny masonry wall. Standard varieties make a good dense perimeter hedge, with orange, cream, or variegated flowers.

Rhus glabra 'Laciniata'

cutleaf smooth sumac

grows 8–12 feet tall and wider

best in zones 3–8

special attributes: Cutleaf smooth sumac is a North American native with suckering stems, an upright, sparsely branched habit, and tropical-looking foliage. Dark green leaves turn brilliant orange-red in autumn. Pointed clusters of furry red fruit top the branches, effective into winter.

design ideas: Place where it can spread unless you are willing to police suckers. Striking alongside evergreens such as Arizona cypress or Taylor juniper and with large grasses such as Wright's sacaton or bull muhly.

related low-water shrubs: Native Rocky Mountain sumac (*Rhus glabra* var. *cismontana*) grows less than half the height. Excellent on slopes and embankments, red fall color, foliage less ferny. Large southwestern native flame sumac (*R. lanceolata*), zones 5–8, grows 15 to 20 tall and almost as wide; also lovely in fall, more heat tolerant than Rocky Mountain sumac.

Ribes odoratum 'Crandall'

clove currant

grows 4–6 feet tall and wide

best in zones 4–7, also zone 8 on the West Coast

special attributes:
This North American native has small, early, trumpet-shaped yellow flowers with a permeating spicy-sweet fragrance, loved by hummingbirds. Fruit of 'Crandall' is larger and sweeter than the straight species, a ½- to ¾-inch shiny black berry appealing to wildlife and human palates. Small lobed foliage turns russet in fall.

design ideas: This casual-looking midsize shrub is ideal for naturalistic gardens, mixed with Apache plume, leadplant, and 'Grey Owl' juniper. Nice amid evergreens to accentuate early yellow flowers and red fall color.

related low-water shrubs: *Ribes odoratum* subsp. *aureum* 'Gwen's Buffalo' is similar on all counts except slightly hardier, to zone 3, and flowers and fruit are a bit smaller.

Rosmarinus officinalis

rosemary

grows 1–3 feet tall and 3–10 feet wide

best in zones 8–10, hardier varieties such as 'Arp', 'Madeline Hill' in zones 6b–10

special attributes: A culinary herb native to the Mediterranean region, rosemary has a dense habit and handsome pinelike green to grayish aromatic foliage. Grows actively during cool spring or fall weather; difficult to establish in summer heat. 'Tuscan Blue' is upright with a compact habit and sapphire blue flowers in early spring; numerous other varieties offer blue, white, or pale pink blossoms; all attract bees. In late fall, cuttings root so easily that they can be stuck directly into the garden.

design ideas: Shears well; good topiary subject. Combine with silver artemisias and cenizas, large cacti and agaves. Plant in roof gardens. Grow against walls in hot sun for extra aroma.

related low-water shrubs: Prostrate rosemary (*Rosmarinus officinalis* var. *prostrata*) drapes over walls, cascades down slopes; branches carry scattering of pale blue flowers fall through winter. 'Lockwood DeForest', 'Huntington Carpet', 'Irene' are popular selections.

Rubus ×tridel 'Benenden'

hybrid boulder raspberry

grows 5–6 feet tall and 6–8 feet wide

best in zones 5–7

special attributes: Hybrid boulder raspberry is one of only a few flowering shrubs adapted to light, dry shade as well as sun. Large roselike white flowers bloom along graceful, arching, sparsely branched stems in late spring for a few weeks, attracting bees. Foliage is lobed and fresh green. Unlike most of its bramble kin, this raspberry does not sucker or have thorns. Fruit is disappointingly dry and inedible. Remove the oldest stems every few years to rejuvenate.

design ideas: Lovely in part shade where the pale flowers and fresh foliage luminesce.

related low-water shrubs: Rocky Mountain native boulder raspberry (*Rubus deliciosus*) is one of the parents of 'Benenden' and is a smaller plant with more modest flowers.

Salvia greggii

autumn sage

grows 2 feet tall and 3 feet wide

best in zones 7–10, 'Wild Thing', 'Furman's Red', 'Ultra Violet' to zones 5b in the West

special attributes: This southwestern subshrub has aromatic foliage and tubular rose, pink, or white flowers with wide lips that attract hummingbirds, butterflies, and bees. Blooms best in cool fall and spring weather. Yellow and coral selections are less cold hardy. 'Pink Preference' and hybrid 'Ultra Violet' (pictured below) have dark purple calyces. Shear to keep compact and vigorous.

design ideas: Nice with large agaves, yuccas, and ceniza. Combine with midsize grasses, verbenas, evening primrose, and silver ponyfoot.

related low-water shrubs: Mount Lemmon sage (*Salvia microphylla*) has leaves with dimpled margins; 'Silke's Dream' and 'Scarlet Spires' are showy hybrids with larger spikes of scarlet blooms. *Salvia regla* makes a lanky, 3-foot shrub with fresh green foliage and orange-red flowers in dense clusters in fall and winter; prefers light shade.

Salvia officinalis

culinary sage

grows 1–2 feet tall and 1–3 feet wide

best in zones 5b–7, also zones 8–10 on the West Coast, short-lived in humid climates

special attributes: Culinary sage is an aromatic gray-leaved herbal subshrub. Lavender-blue flowers in loose spikes bloom in spring or early summer, attracting bees. Narrow- and round-leafed, prostrate, variegated, and purple-leafed selections are available; colored foliage selections are a bit less hardy. The hybrid cultivar 'Newe Ya'ar' is the most heat tolerant.

design ideas: Good at path's edge. Contrasts with fine-textured santolina, rosemary, and lavender in an aromatic melee. Mingle with 'Shimmer' evening primrose, perky Sue, yarrow, dianthus, hop-flowered oreganos, penstemons, skullcaps, scarlet betony, and hummingbird trumpet.

related low-water shrubs: In mild, dry climates (zones 8–10 on the West Coast), pungent blue-flowered *Salvia clevelandii* and blindingly silver *S. apiana*, along with larger, bicolored blue and black-purple *S. semiatrata*, are standouts. In harsher dry zones (5–8 in the West), mauve-bracted *S. pachyphylla* and blue-flowered *S. dorrii* make silvery subshrubs, while *S. chamaedryoides* (zones 7–10 in the West) is the smallest, a lax mound of tiny gray leaves with cobalt blue flowers.

Santolina chamaecyparissus

lavender cotton

grows 1–2 feet tall and 2–4 feet wide

best in zones 6–10, herbaceous perennial in zone 5 in the West, resents humid heat

special attributes: This aromatic subshrub has finely divided silver-gray foliage in dense, frothy-looking mounds. Small buttonlike gold flowers top the bushes in late spring to midsummer, depending on climate, and attract bees and butterflies. In hot climates, best planted and pruned in cool spring or fall weather.

design ideas: Makes a traditional edging for formal herb and knot gardens; shears well. Combine with yuccas, agaves, smaller grasses, verbenas, evening primrose, hummingbird trumpet, leadwort, or dwarf sedums. Plant in roof gardens.

related low-water shrubs: Green santolina (*Santolina rosmarinifolia*, formerly *S. virens*) has aromatic, feathery bright green foliage and pale yellow flowers.

Seriphidium filifolium (formerly *Artemisia filifolia*)

thread-leaf sage

grows 3–4 feet tall and wide

best in zones 3–7 in regions with low humidity

special attributes: Aromatic, thread-thin silver foliage cloaks this western North American native, giving it a unique, ghostly, feathery presence. Must have sun and not be crowded by other shrubs or will get leggy and floppy. Cut back by a third in early spring to keep compact and vigorous.

design ideas: Beautiful with a dark evergreen backdrop of pines or allowed to shimmer near Apache plume and blue joint fir in a sunny, backlit shrub border.

related low-water shrubs: Western sage (*Seriphidium tridentatum*) is the iconic, highly aromatic sagebrush of the Intermountain West, with toothed darker gray foliage. It, like threadleaf sage, must be grown very dry and pruned hard to stay attractive.

Syringa ×chinensis

Chinese lilac

grows 10–15 feet tall and wide

best in zones 4–7, also zone 8 on the West Coast

special attributes: Chinese lilac is a large, dense shrub with tidy fresh green foliage and masses of airy lavender-blue flower clusters in spring, sometimes visited by bees and early butterflies. An almost white form and a rich purple called 'Saugeana' are available.

design ideas: Makes a fine hedge or screen; mixes well with other large shrubs such as western mock orange, smoke bush, and beauty bush.

related low-water shrubs: One of Chinese lilac's parents, common lilac (*Syringa vulgaris*), is slightly hardier and more fragrant but has an ungainly, sparse habit and coarser, less attractive foliage. It can be invasive in certain regions. The other parent, Persian lilac, is a lovely, almost sterile shrub about a third smaller but with disappointing fragrance. *Syringa oblata*, early lilac, looks like common lilac with better amber to burgundy fall color and earlier bloom that can be more prone to frost damage.

Teucrium fruticans

shrub germander

grows 4 feet tall and wide

best in zones 8–10, resents humid heat

special attributes: Shrub germander is a twiggy silver-gray subshrub with small blue flowers that appear in fall and winter. 'Compactum' has pale blue flowers and a dense habit; 'Azureum' is more open with intense cobalt blue flowers (pictured close-up). Bees flock to the plant, and butterflies come as well. Grows actively during cool spring or fall weather; difficult to establish in summer heat.

design ideas: Clip as a hedge or topiary. Makes a nice contrast to rosemary or harmonizes in a silver-and-blue composition with large agaves and silver ponyfoot.

related low-water shrubs: Waxy green leaves and wine-colored blossoms make smaller, shrubby wall germander (*Teucrium chamaedrys*), zones 6–10, a popular low edging.

Perennials

Low-water perennials return each year, bringing diversity and excitement to gardens with their luxuriant flowering effects and distinctive foliage. In colder regions these plants take on a special importance, often filling roles typically occupied by subshrubs and shrubs. The perennials we've described require an annual cleanup in fall or early spring to remove old duff and prepare for the growing season but otherwise need little care.

Achillea 'Moonshine'

'Moonshine' yarrow

grows 18 inches tall and 2 feet wide

best in zones 3–10, resents extreme heat

special attributes: This yarrow is a long-blooming hybrid with ferny silver foliage that sets off flat-topped lemon yellow flower clusters. Bloom time is early to mid summer. Worth growing for its foliage alone. Unlike the majority of yarrows, it does not spread or self-sow. Excellent cut and dried flower; attracts butterflies.

design ideas: 'Moonshine' yarrow is superb in evening gardens alongside the pale flowers and foliage of 'Shimmer' evening primrose, white daisies of *Tanacetum niveum* or *T. cinerariifolium*, and silvery blue agaves, yuccas, and sotols. Also lovely with grasses, 'Walker's Low' catmint, and lavender.

related low-water perennials: Gray-leafed, nonspreading yarrows include pale yellow 'Anthea' and coppery 'Terracotta'. Dwarf species of yarrow *Achillea serbica*, *A. ageratifolia*, and *A. ×kelleri* also have silvery gray foliage, resent extreme heat as well as humidity.

Agastache rupestris

sunset hyssop

grows 18–24 inches tall and 2–3 feet wide

best in zones 4b–10 with hot summers, prefers low humidity

special attributes: A southwestern native, sunset hyssop opens tubular soft orange flower spikes from midsummer until frost, attracting hummingbirds and sphinx moths. Narrow gray-green foliage complements the flowers and smells strongly of licorice. Cut back to a few inches before growth resumes to promote strong, bushy growth. Avoid fall planting in zones 4–7.

design ideas: Beautiful with grasses, Russian sage, blue mist spirea, rabbitbrush, or among bold yuccas, sotols, and agaves.

related low-water perennials: Agastache species and hybrids range from 1 to 4 feet in height and are usually only hardy to zone 6; most lack the nice habit and fine-textured foliage of sunset hyssop. Hardier and among the most attractive are large 'Orange Flare', 'Desert Sunrise', and rose red 'Ava' (all hybrids), and more compact *Agastache cana* 'Rosita' and apricot *A. aurantiaca* 'Coronado'.

Alyssum montanum

mountain alyssum

grows 6 inches tall and 15 inches wide

best in zones 3–7, prefers low humidity but adaptable

special attributes: This low-growing, short-lived perennial is among the first to bloom in the spring, with masses of small golden flowers for well over a month. Tiny gray-green foliage looks good all year, forming a lax mound. Cut back spent flowers for bushiness and vigor. Self-sows mildly. Attracts early foraging bees and butterflies.

design ideas: Mountain alyssum makes a bright, neat edge plant. Pretty with small spring-flowering bulbs such as species tulips and grape hyacinths. Mingles comfortably with cacti.

related low-water perennials: *Alyssum markgrafii* is twice the height, with deeper yellow flowers on upright stems in late spring and early summer. This short-lived, mildly self-sowing perennial is a zone less hardy and tolerates heat and humidity better.

Asclepias tuberosa

butterfly weed

grows 18–24 inches tall and wide

best in zones 4–8 with hot summers

special attributes: This widespread North American native has orange —or more rarely yellow or red—flat-topped flower clusters for several weeks in midsummer, beloved of butterflies and bees. Bold lime green foliage in a bushy habit turns gold and maroon in fall. Large seedpods hold dark brown seeds with silken white parachutes. Long lived, self-sows. Prefers sandy soils but clay-adapted strains are available. Good cut flower. Feeds caterpillars of monarch and queen butterflies.

design ideas: Superb meadow plant that can compete with bunchgrasses such as blue grama or blue fescue. Lovely with Indian blanket and lavender.

Baptisia minor (formerly *Baptisia australis* var. *minor*)

wild indigo

grows 18–36 inches tall and wide

best in zones 4–8 with hot summers

special attributes: This deep-rooted, long-lived perennial is native to central North America. Thick stalks emerge midspring and unfurl to bushy branched stems covered with lovely cloverlike gray-green leaves. In May or June, large lupinelike spikes of lavender-blue blossoms open, attracting bees and bumblebees. Foliage and ripening inflated black seedpods remain attractive through summer except in very hot climates. Feeds caterpillars of several species of blue, sulphur, and indigo butterflies as well as the dogface.

design ideas: Mingle with grasses as a standout in prairie gardens. Nice with yarrow, oriental poppies, or Jupiter's beard.

related low-water perennials: 'Purple Smoke' is a slightly larger garden hybrid with elegant charcoal gray stems and tall spikes of light purple flowers. *Baptisia bracteata* is the other low-water wild indigo species, slightly smaller and less bushy, with large, drooping creamy flower spikes in late spring.

Calylophus hartwegii

sundrop

grows 1 foot tall and 2 feet wide

best in zones 5–10 with low humidity

special attributes: This long-blooming southwestern native evening primrose peaks in summer in colder regions and in spring and fall in hotter climates. The large luminous yellow flowers turn peach as they fade. Habit is lax.

design ideas: Mingle sundrops with small grasses such as blue grama, Mexican feather grass, sheep's fescue, or Indian rice grass. Their mounds also drape nicely over walls and rocks. Combine with blackfoot daisy, plains skullcap, blue sage, desert bluebells, cacti, and smaller agaves and yuccas.

related low-water perennials: Prairie sundrop (*Calylophus serrulatus*) is smaller in all ways, hardy to zone 4, and best suited to cold-winter climates. Look-alike *C. drummondii* tolerates heat and humidity. Lavender-leaf sundrop (*C. lavandulifolius*) is the most compact and adapted to zones 4–7 with low humidity.

Centranthus ruber

Jupiter's beard, Greek valerian

grows 2 feet tall and 3 feet wide

best in zones 4–7, can be invasive in mild maritime regions

special attributes: An old-fashioned cottage garden plant, Jupiter's beard blooms for many weeks in late spring and summer. Its airy rose red or white flower clusters attract butterflies. May self-sow abundantly if not deadheaded; reblooms when cut back. Blue-green foliage remains attractive all year.

design ideas: Excellent flower garden plant alongside penstemons, catmint, and bearded iris. Intermingle in casual shrub plantings with artemisias, thread-leaf sage, and Apache plume.

Dalea purpurea (formerly *Petalostemon purpureum*)

purple prairie clover

grows 12–18 inches tall and wide

best in zones 3–7

special attributes:
This long-lived prairie native has an airy upright habit; its plump, knobby rose-purple flower spikes hover on wiry stems in midsummer, attracting bees, bumblebees, and butterflies. Self-sows a little. Feeds caterpillars of the dogface butterfly.

design ideas: Ideal with smaller grasses, Indian blanket, butterfly weed, prairie petunia, and gayfeather in a low-water meadow planting. A jaunty midsummer accent amid sprawling prairie winecup.

Datura wrightii

thorn apple, angel's trumpet

grows 2–3 feet tall, 3–5 feet wide

best in zones 6–10, grow as an annual in colder regions

special attributes: Thorn apple is a bushy tap-rooted southwestern native with thick stems and large velvety gray-green leaves. Huge funnel-shaped white flowers, jasmine scented and sometimes tinged purple, open at dusk all summer, attracting sphinx moths and bees. These ripen to large, prickly, burr-like seedpods.

design ideas: Plant near courtyard walls, along sidewalks, by entryways where evening flowers and fragrance can be enjoyed. Handsome with large yuccas and agaves.

Dianthus gratianopolitanus

cheddar pink

grows 6–12 inches tall and 15–18 inches wide

best in zones 4–8, also zones 9–10 on the West Coast

special attributes: A very heat-tolerant dianthus, unlike most, the cheddar pink makes beautiful blue-gray foliage mounds year-round. Several selections are available with lightly fragrant pink, rose, crimson, white, or bicolored flowers that bloom from late spring into early summer with some rebloom later on, attracting butterflies and sphinx moths. May self-sow a little. 'Bath's Pink' is a pale pink, longer lived, more humidity tolerant selection. 'Tiny Rubies' (pictured) is especially dwarf, with double flowers like miniature carnations.

design ideas: Nice edge plant, also favored in rock gardens. Combine with ice plants, small sedums, cushion phlox, sheep's fescue, and plains skullcap for a low-growing tapestry garden. Plant in roof gardens.

related low-water perennials: Jasmine pink (*Dianthus petraeus* subsp. *noeanus*) has highly fragrant white flowers in midsummer. It is long lived and also heat tolerant. Foliage forms a prickly evergreen dome, emerald green rather than gray-blue.

Echinacea angustifolia

prairie coneflower, blacksamson

grows 12–24 inches tall and 8–16 inches wide

best in zones 3–8, worth trying in zones 9–10 on the West Coast

special attributes: This widespread prairie native has rough, hairy gray-green leaves in tufts from thick roots. Daisy flowers appear June to July with pink to rose-purple rays around dome-shaped central orange disks; attract butterflies, bees. Finches eat ripe seeds. Favored medicinal plant of the Plains Indians.

design ideas: Interplant among grasses. Combine with fine-textured perennials like purple prairie clover or Mexicali penstemon. Allow seed heads to stand through winter.

related low-water perennials: Pale coneflower (*Echinacea pallida*) of the central plains is taller, with narrow drooping rays, hybridizes with *E. angustifolia* where ranges overlap.

Eriogonum umbellatum

sulfur flower, buckwheat

grows 12 inches tall and 18 inches wide

best in zones 3–8 with low humidity, also zones 9–10 on the West Coast

special attributes: Sulfur flower is a western native with year-round beauty. In late spring and early summer, rounded clusters of yellow papery flowers draw bees. As these dry and form seeds, they often turn reddish. The low-growing mat of leathery dark green foliage takes on rusty maroon hues in winter. Feeds caterpillars of the gorgon copper butterfly.

design ideas: Lovely with any blue-flowered penstemon, and with cacti and yuccas. Excellent for evening gardens with its luminescent flowers. Good roof garden plant.

related low-water perennials: Tiny spring-blooming *Eriogonum ovalifolium* has silver leaves and creamy pompom flowers. *Eriogonum niveum* has snowy clouds of late summer and autumn flowers; *E. wrightii*'s bloom is a peachy fawn color. Yellow *E. allenii* is the most tolerant of high humidity.

Eryngium planum

blue sea holly

grows 18–30 inches tall and 18 inches wide

best in zones 4–7, also zones 8–10 on the West Coast

special attributes: A stiff upright spray of spiny silvery blue flowers rises up from blue sea holly's shiny rich green foliage rosette in midsummer for many weeks. Short lived, self-sows. Excellent cut and dried flower. Attracts bees and beneficial wasps.

design ideas: Sea holly makes a welcome high summer combination with airy grasses such as alkali sacaton or European feather grass, and rosy lavender pincushion flower.

related low-water perennials: Blue-flowered *Eryngium amethystinum* is more compact, later blooming, and with silver-veined, spiny, deeply cleft foliage. *Eryngium maritimum* is silvery turquoise in leaf and flower, and sprawls. Both are hardy to zone 5.

Gaillardia aristata

Indian blanket

grows 12–18 inches tall and wide

best in zones 3–8, also zones 9–10 on the West Coast, short lived in the Southeast

special attributes: This western native blooms for months if kept dead-headed. The species is longer lived than the more common hybrids. 'Amber Wheels' is extra floriferous with butter-scotch-colored daisies with red centers. Self-sows some. Bees and butterflies visit the cheerful flowers.

design ideas: Indian blanket has an open habit with sparse foliage, so looks best in naturalistic plantings. Pairs well with grasses, pen-stemons, and sundrops.

related low-water perennials: *Gaillardia ×grandiflora* 'Goblin' and 'Arizona Sun' are under a foot tall and perform better, with a longer lifespan and with more flowers over a longer season, than other hybrids. Their flowers are red with a yellow rim. Their short stems and mounded habit are tidy but they lack the prairie wildflower appeal of their parents.

Helianthus maximiliani

Maximilian sunflower

grows 5–10 feet tall and 3–5 feet wide or more

best in zones 4–8, also zones 9–10 in the West

special attributes: This robust sunflower native to the Great Plains grows from long-lived spreading rootstocks. Upright stems carry rough-textured green leaves; golden yellow daisies appear for several weeks in late summer or fall, attracting goldfinches and butterflies. Earlier flowering selections such as 'Dakota Sunshine' are best for northern gardens. Feeds caterpillars of the bordered patch butterfly.

design ideas: Plant as a screen near walls or fences. Combine with tall grasses, azure sage, sunset hyssop, 'Taylor' juniper.

related low-water perennials: *Helianthus ×laetiflorus* 'Lemon Queen' bears soft yellow daisies July to August on bright green bushes 5 feet tall and wide, good cut flower. Willow-leaf sunflower (*H. salicifolius*) flowers late summer or fall with graceful 5-foot stems carrying narrow threadlike leaves.

Iris orientalis (formerly *Iris ochroleuca*)

white spuria iris, Turkish iris

grows 3 feet tall and 2–4 feet wide

best in zones 4–8, also zones 9–10 on the West Coast

special attributes: This is a long-lived heirloom iris with elegantly narrow foliage and tall stems bearing vanilla-scented white flowers blotched yellow. Blossoms attract bees, appear after tall bearded irises bloom. Unlike those, resents disturbance; divide spuria iris infrequently if at all.

design ideas: Cottage garden plant, pretty with artemisias. Foliage good in modern designs; combine with feather grass.

related low-water perennials: Similar spuria iris are available in blue, purple, yellow, unusual earth tones, and bicolor cultivars. Algerian iris (*Iris unguicularis*), zones 7–10, with slender foliage to 18 inches tall, sends up fragrant blue or white flowers on short stems from November to March and thrives in sun or shade.

Liatris punctata

prairie gayfeather

grows 12–15 inches tall and 15 inches wide

best in zones 3–7 with low humidity

special attributes: This long-lived shortgrass prairie native blooms in late summer, drawing butterflies and hummingbirds. The bouquet of upright rose-purple spikes is clothed in leathery narrow dark green foliage. May self-sow. The most drought-resistant gayfeather species.

design ideas: Beautiful with smaller grasses such as blue grama or little bluestem. Also combines well with hop-flowered oregano and purple mountain savory.

related low-water perennials: *Liatris squarrosa* and *L. mucronata* are more heat and humidity tolerant. *Liatris aspera* is the tallest water-thrifty gayfeather at 3–4 feet in height.

Limonium platyphyllum (formerly *Limonium latifolium*)

sea lavender

grows 2 feet tall and wide

best in zones 4–7, also zones 8–10 on the West Coast

special attributes: Sea lavender blooms in a cloud of tiny papery light purple flowers, adding an airy touch in the late summer garden. The flowers dry well both in garden and vase. Large tonguelike, leathery evergreen leaves lie low to the ground. Beneficial wasps and bees frequent the flowers.

design ideas: The billowing flowers mingle well with midsize grasses, chartreuse and rose bracted oreganos, or dramatic white angel's trumpet. The plant's form can help soften a corner, edge, retaining wall, or rocky slope.

related low-water plants: *Limonium gmelinii* has more upright sprays of purple flowers ideal for narrower spaces, later to bloom. German statice (*Goniolimon tataricum*) is the earliest to bloom, smaller, and white flowered.

Linum lewisii

western blue flax

grows 18 inches tall and wide

best in zones 3–7, also zones 8–10 on the West Coast

special attributes: This long-blooming, short-lived western native smothers itself in sky blue flowers in late spring and early summer. It has a wispy, wild demeanor with scanty needlelike blue-green foliage. White-flowered forms are available. Cut back the top half of the plant after bloom unless thousands of seedlings are desired.

design ideas: Pair with other pretty thugs: California poppies, Mexican feather grass, and pink evening primrose (*Oenothera speciosa*) in naturalistic areas or interplant among shrubs and large yuccas.

related low-water perennials: Slightly smaller *Linum narbonense* has fewer, larger, deeper blue flowers. Yellow-flowered flax species—*Linum flavum, L. bulgaricum, L. tauricum, L. capitatum, L. dolomiticum*—are longer lived, have larger, greener foliage, and grow to about half the stature. All of these species seed less prolifically.

Melampodium leucanthemum

blackfoot daisy

grows 8–10 inches tall and 12–14 inches wide

best in zones 6–8, worth trying in zone 9 in the West

special attributes: A mounding southwestern and Great Plains native, blackfoot daisy is covered spring to fall with small white daisies. Young plants are more sensitive to extra water at establishment than most plants.

design ideas: Combine with cacti, yuccas, and agaves. Plant in rock gardens and strips along sidewalks. Cheerful white daisies pair well with most small water-wise perennials.

related low-water perennials: Rocky Mountain zinnia (*Zinnia grandiflora*), zones 4–7, is native to high elevations in the Southwest and has a more lax habit. It bears persistent papery golden orange flowers midsummer into fall.

Mirabilis multiflora

desert four o'clock

grows 18 inches tall and 48 inches wide

best in zones 4–8 in the West

special attributes: Sprouting annually from a huge underground tuber, this southwestern native forms sprawling mounds of lush blue-green foliage with daily crops of funnel-shaped magenta flowers opening in the afternoon through much of the summer. Attracts hummingbirds and sphinx moths, whose caterpillars it also feeds. Self-sows mildly.

design ideas: Combine with yuccas and agaves. Nice with evening primrose and angel's trumpet in evening gardens.

related low-water perennials: Common four o'clock or wonder of Peru (*Mirabilis jalapa*), zones 7–10, is a self-seeding heirloom with branched leafy stems and long-tubed flowers in shades of yellow, rose, purple, or unusual variegated blends. White and yellow strains can be especially fragrant.

Nepeta racemosa 'Walker's Low'

big catmint

grows 18 inches tall and 36 inches wide

best in zones 4–8, also zones 9–10 on the West Coast

special attributes: This nonseeding, nonspreading catmint is a pollinator's mecca, drawing bees, bumblebees, sphinx moths, and hummingbirds to its misty blue flower spikes for two months in late spring and early summer. Small gray-green foliage is aromatic when touched. Some rebloom occurs in late summer and fall; cut back spent spikes to keep plant from opening up in the center.

design ideas: Looks good with almost any plant; especially nice with tall penstemons, evening primroses, and bearded iris. Good roof garden plant.

related low-water perennials: *Nepeta* ×*faassenii* 'Select Blue' is half the size and a paler blue, also mercifully nonseeding and nonspreading, unlike common catmint. It begins bloom a few weeks before 'Walker's Low'.

Oenothera macrocarpa subsp. *fremontii* 'Shimmer'

'Shimmer' evening primrose

grows 4–8 inches tall and 12–15 inches wide

best in zones 4–8, also zones 9–10 on the West Coast

special attributes: This evening primrose is a Great Plains native with narrow gray-green leaves making sprawling, fine-textured mats. Large pale yellow flowers appear in summer, opening at dusk, attracting sphinx moths with sweet fragrance. The plant feeds their caterpillars. 'Shimmer' is an extra silvery, grassy-leafed selection made in the authors' Colorado garden.

design ideas: Plant as edging or low silvery foil for other perennials, cacti, and yuccas. Ideal for evening gardens with silver-leafed and white-flowered companions. Place along paths or in courtyards to enjoy fragrance. Good for roof gardens.

related low-water perennials: Missouri evening primrose (*Oenothera macrocarpa* var. *macrocarpa*) of the eastern Great Plains has oblong green leaves; *O. macrocarpa* subsp. *incana*, sold as 'Silver Blade', has gray foliage, while similarly silvery 'Comanche Campfire' has added red stems. All these self-sow mildly.

Origanum libanoticum and hybrids

hop-flowered oregano

grows 12–15 inches tall and 18 inches wide

best in zones 5–10, resents humid heat

special attributes: From midsummer into fall, masses of shrimplike, papery chartreuse bracts dangle from this plant's lax, wiry stems clothed in tidy rounded gray-green leaves. The bracts enclose small rose-purple flowers for several weeks and persist into fall, freshening the late-season garden with their soft color. Attracts bees. Self-sows mildly.

design ideas: Looks best cascading over rocks, on walls and slopes or along paths. The pale bracts shimmer at dusk, lovely with evening primroses. Roof garden plant.

related low-water perennials: Several species and hybrids of hop-flowered oregano exist. Most are less hardy, only to zones 6 or 7. 'Pilgrim' and 'Amethyst Falls' (pictured) are two beautiful hardier hybrids. *Origanum rotundifolium* (zone 5) has the largest bracts, often tinged pink.

Papaver atlanticum 'Flore Pleno'

double-flowered Spanish poppy

grows 18 inches tall and wide

best in zones 4–7, also zones 8–10 on the West Coast, short lived in humid climates

special attributes: A blue-green hairy foliage rosette sets off a parade of double poppy flowers in soft orange hovering on thin but sturdy stems. Bloom continues for more than two months starting in late spring, especially when periodically deadheaded. Bees enjoy this plant. Spanish poppy self-sows a little and seedlings of the double form also have double flowers.

design ideas: The orange flowers are lovely with the blue blossoms of flax, catmint, and many penste-mons, and the blue leaves of sheep's fescue.

Papaver orientale

oriental poppy

grows 2–3 feet tall and 4 feet wide

best in zones 3–7, also zones 8–9 on the West Coast, resents humid heat

special attributes: Heart-stopping huge goblets in shades of red, orange, pink, peach, lavender, or white bloom for a couple of weeks in late spring. Bees work feverishly amid the pollen-rich dark stamens. This perennial gets more floriferous each year. Profuse hairy gray-green foliage dies down in midsummer, reemerging as a resting rosette in autumn. Good cut flower.

design ideas: Because of their large size and summer disappearing act, place oriental poppies behind perennials with a longer seasonal presence to hide their lapses. Or plant them among xeric shrubs such as 'Cheyenne' mock orange, blue mist spirea, or 'Powis Castle' artemisia. Grow them along a fence with another seasonal giant, Maximilian sunflower, for a fun two-season show.

Penstemon barbatus

scarlet bugler

grows 18 inches to 5 feet tall in bloom and 18 inches wide

best in zones 4–8, short lived in humid heat

special attributes: This western native is tall and airy in bloom, with most foliage staying in ground-hugging rosettes. Red tubular flowers draw hummingbirds for weeks in early summer. Deadhead to promote vigor. Pink, coral, and yellow selections are more compact at 2 feet tall.

design ideas: The tall red form is shown off best alongside yuccas, sotols, and agaves, or bulky grasses such as Wright's sacaton. Combine more demure selections with catmint, blue flax, or pyrethrum daisy.

related low-water perennials: Firecracker penstemon (*Penstemon eatonii*) is half the height of scarlet bugler and blooms red in the spring for several weeks, attracting the first hummingbirds. *Penstemon rostriflorus* (formerly *P. bridgesii*) is a long-blooming red hummingbird magnet that flowers the second half of the summer. It is one third the height of scarlet bugler, with a shrubbier habit.

Penstemon pinifolius

pineleaf penstemon

grows 8–15 inches tall and wide

best in zones 4–8, also zones 9–10 on the West Coast, one of most adaptable penstemons

special attributes: This long-lived western native has fresh green needlelike foliage in a dense tussock. Plants bloom for many weeks in summer; hummingbirds relish the nectar. The typical orange-red–flowered form takes on burgundy foliage hues in winter. Soft yellow selections have lighter green leaves all year. Blends of red and yellow on the same plant, such as 'Shades of Mango' (pictured), are also available.

design ideas: In bold groupings this plant lives up to its other common name, prairie fire penstemon. Its attractive habit and evergreen foliage make it ideal as an edge or foreground plant.

Compact enough to blend into rock gardens or with small cacti. Lovely in naturalistic plantings with manzanitas and low-growing conifers as well as in more colorful combinations with plains skullcap or evening primrose. Good for roof gardens.

Penstemon Mexicali hybrids

Mexicali penstemon

grows 18 inches tall and 24 inches wide

best in zones 4–8

special attributes: Among the longest blooming and most persistent of the often ephemeral penstemon clan, these hybrids of North American parentage offer tubular flowers in crimson, pink, purple, lavender, and white. Bushy and well clothed in shiny bright-green foliage, Mexicali penstemons also have a better habit than their cousins. Bees and hummingbirds savor the flowers. Bloom begins in early summer, continuing until frost if spent spikes are cut back periodically. Selected color forms are available, such as 'Red Rocks', 'Pikes Peak Purple', and 'Shadow Mountain', but seed strains are often just as good. All self-sow a bit.

design ideas: These hybrids look good with almost anything. Lovely with the fluffy pinkish seed heads of Apache plume and with silver or blue plants of any sort.

Penstemon strictus

Rocky Mountain penstemon

grows 18–30 inches tall and wide

best in zones 3–8 with low humidity

special attributes: One of the longer lived of the penstemon clan, this western native opens abundant indigo flowers in thick spikes for several weeks in late spring and early summer. Shiny emerald green foliage stays fresh looking year-round. Deadhead after bloom to promote vigor. Bees, bumblebees, and hummingbirds relish the blossoms. Self-sows mildly.

design ideas: Stunning with Jupiter's beard, snow daisy, other penstemons, silver sage, and striped bearded iris.

related low-water perennials: *Penstemon mensarum*, *P. neomexicanus*, *P. cyananthus*, *P. glaber*, and *P. speciosus* are other beautiful large blue-flowered, spring-blooming penstemons but not as widely adaptable as Rocky Mountain penstemon.

Ratibida columnifera

prairie coneflower, Mexican hat

grows 15–24 inches tall and 18 inches wide

best in zones 4–10

special attributes: This central North American native sends up profuse daisies with drooping rays and prominent centers. Golden yellow and vibrant rust red forms are available in the trade. Flowers open late spring to fall on slender stems with bright green cleft leaves. Attracts butterflies; seeds favored by finches. Self-sows abundantly.

design ideas: Combine with little bluestem, Mexican feather grass, or blue grama in meadow plantings. Consorts well with Indian blanket and butterfly weed for bright floral effects.

related low-water perennials: Yellow coneflower (*Ratibida pinnata*), zones 3–8, is native to the eastern Great Plains, reaches 4 feet tall, bears large yellow flowers with dark cones and tapered pendant rays in mid to late summer, and needs a bit more water to thrive.

Ruellia humilis (formerly *Ruellia ciliosa*)

wild petunia

grows 16–24 inches tall and wide

best in zones 4–8

special attributes: Wild petunia is a widespread North American native with sparsely felted gray-green leaves. Showy lilac funnel-shaped flowers open daily from late spring to fall, attracting bees and butterflies. Self-sows mildly; seedlings are hard to pull out. Feeds caterpillars of the buckeye butterfly.

design ideas: Combine with wine cup and blue grama or little bluestem in a short prairie planting. Pair with ivory sedge and hop-flowered oregano in dry shade.

related low-water perennials: Dwarf Mexican petunia (*Ruellia brittoniana* 'Katie'), zones 7–10, bears lush green lance-shaped leaves in low tufts with large purple flowers (also available in white or pink). Large forms of *R. brittoniana* spread by underground stems and can be invasive. Southwestern desert natives *R. peninsularis* and *R. californica*, zones 9–10, make semi-evergreen subshrubs with purple flowers.

Salvia argentea

silver sage

grows 2 feet tall and 18 inches wide

best in zones 4–8, also zones 9–10 on the West Coast, short lived in humid heat

special attributes: The large, hairy, glistening foliage of silver sage forms a bulky rosette, the main reason to grow this plant. In early summer, candelabras of white flowers arise for a short period, attracting bees and bumblebees. Remove flower stems when finished to enjoy the lovely foliage. Self-sows a little.

design ideas: Combine with wine cup, hummingbird trumpet, or 'Select Blue' catmint. Intermingle with yuccas, leadplant, threadleaf sage, and Russian sage in chaparral style, or play on a silver theme with snow in summer and seafoam sage.

related low-water perennials: Platinum sage (*Salvia daghestanica*), zones 5–7 in the West and zones 8–10 on the West Coast, makes a ground-hugging mat of hairy silver foliage with short spikes of large lavender-blue flowers in early summer. It resents excess rain and humidity.

Salvia farinacea 'Texas Violet'

'Texas Violet' blue sage, hardy mealy-cup sage

grows 2–3 feet tall and 2 feet wide

best in zones 6–10, worth trying in zone 5b in the West

special attributes: This southwestern native sage blooms late spring to fall. Pliant stems from the woody root carry aromatic gray-green leaves. Spikes of two-lipped violet flowers, held in silvery calyces, attract butterflies and bees.

design ideas: Combine with yuccas, agaves, and cacti. Plant with California poppies, evening primrose, and butterfly weed for a long season of color.

related low-water perennials: Taller prairie native azure sage (*S. azurea* var. *grandiflora*) blooms late and is often floppy in the garden, needing support. It has cobalt blue flowers, sky blue in the form 'Nekan', hardy in zones 4–9. Texan *S. reptans* is similar but with willowlike foliage, hardy in zones 6–9.

Satureja montana subsp. *illyrica*

purple mountain savory

grows 8–12 inches tall and 12–18 inches wide

best in zones 4–8, also zones 9–10 on the West Coast, resents humid heat

special attributes: This plant's tidy, fine-textured bright green mound of foliage is a delight amid the more common dusty gray-greens of many low-water plants. The plant bursts into rich purple, bee-beloved bloom in late summer for several weeks. Cut back in late winter to keep bushy. Evergreen in milder climates. Self-sows a little.

design ideas: Low-growing plant with great texture and late season flower color for rock gardens, edges, tapestry plantings, and roof gardens. Combine with sundrops, hummingbird trumpet, prairie gayfeather, or hop-flowered oregano.

Scabiosa columbaria

compact pincushion flower

grows 15–18 inches tall and 12–15 inches wide

best in zones 4–8, also zones 9–10 on the West Coast, short lived in humid heat

special attributes: This tireless bloomer opens dome-shaped lavender or pink flowers on wiry stems for months on end if deadheaded now and again. Butterflies and bees relish the flowers. 'Butterfly Blue' and 'Pink Mist' are more compact selections. Excellent cut flower. Self-sows mildly.

design ideas: The airy flowers blend with smaller grasses such as blue fescue, little bluestem, or Mexican feather grass. Combine with sundrops, butterfly weed, checkermallow, dwarf yellow onion, or yellow-flowered selections of pineleaf penstemon. Good roof garden plant.

Scutellaria resinosa

prairie skullcap

grows 8 inches tall and 10–12 inches wide

best in zones 4–8, also zones 9–10 on the West Coast

special attributes: Prairie skullcap is a native of the Great Plains that grows in a flowery mound of rounded gray-green leaves. Small purple blossoms smother stems from late spring through summer. Short lived; self-sows moderately. 'Smoky Hills' is a larger-flowered selection.

design ideas: Combine with smaller cacti, yuccas, and agaves. Plant with sundrops, perky Sue, pineleaf penstemon, and blackfoot daisy on slopes, in rock gardens, and in narrow strips along sidewalks.

related low-water perennials: *Scutellaria wrightii* (zones 6–9) is a nearly indistinguishable, tidy native of the southern plains. 'Violet Cloud' (zones 6–9) is a light lavender hybrid with pink skullcap, *S. suffrutescens* (zones 7–9), which has everblooming rose red or cream flowers and a neat shrubby habit and is longer lived, making it ideal for roof gardens.

Sidalcea malviflora

checkermallow

grows 18–24 inches tall and 12–18 inches wide

best in zones 4–8, also zones 8–10 on the West Coast

special attributes: This western native blooms for well over a month in summer with large pink, rose, or white flowers on spikes. Lush shiny green lobed foliage belies its water thriftiness. Self-sows mildly. Bees and hummingbirds visit the flowers. Good cut flower. Remove spent flower stalks for rebloom and to encourage basal overwintering foliage.

design ideas: For a cottage garden look, plant with larkspur, wine cup, pincushion flower, and sea lavender. Its upright, airy carriage also blends well with smaller grasses.

related low-water perennials: Hybrid selections are taller and not as drought resistant as the species. Musk mallow (*Malva moschata*) is bushier and less upright.

Stachys coccinea

Texas betony, scarlet betony

grows 8–12 inches tall and 12–18 inches wide

best in zones 6–10, worth trying in zone 5b in the West

special attributes: Texas betony is a southwestern native with serrated green heart-shaped leaves in bushy mounds. In mild climates it remains evergreen in winter, taking on purple tints. A profuse parade of short spikes of tubular scarlet flowers carries on all summer, attracting hummingbirds.

design ideas: Combine with cacti, yuccas, and agaves. Plant with leadwort, sedums, blue fescue, blackfoot daisy, and santolina. Good in rock gardens, narrow strips along sidewalks, and roof gardens.

related low-water perennials: *Stachys albotomentosa* 'Hidalgo', zones 8–10, has larger felted sage green leaves and salmon flowers.

Symphyotrichum oblongifolium (formerly *Aster oblongifolius, A. kumleinii*)

aromatic aster

grows 1–3 feet tall and wide

best in zones 3–8, also zones 9–10 on the West Coast

special attributes: This widespread North American aster has tiny slender leaves that are aromatic when crushed. Keeps a tidy mounded form. Lavender yellow-centered daisies cover the plant in fall, attracting bees and butterflies. Finches relish the seed. Self-sows abundantly. Heirloom in the South. 'Raydon's Favorite', 'October Skies', and 'Fanny' are lavender; 'Dream of Beauty' is light sugar pink with a dwarf spreading habit.

design ideas: Combine with silver spike grass, artemisia, rabbitbrush, and Maximilian sunflower. Beautiful with the red fall foliage of sumac or golden currant.

related low-water perennials: Widespread North American native heath aster (*Symphyotrichum ericoides*) makes 2-feet-tall-and-wide mounds of intricately branched stems and tiny leaves smothered with white flowers in autumn. 'Snow Flurry' is an extra dwarf selection. Lavender and pink forms are also available.

Tanacetum cinerariifolium

pyrethrum daisy

grows 15–18 inches tall and wide

best in zones 4–8, also zones 9–10 on the West Coast

special attributes: Pure white daisies hover on wiry stems above handsome mounds of incised gray-green foliage for several weeks in early summer. Foliage remains attractive most of the year. Self-sows mildly. A low-water, refined-looking, well-behaved alternative to ox-eye and Shasta daisies. Source of a natural insecticide.

design ideas: Looks good with almost anything, especially penstemons and feather grass. Lovely in an evening garden with sulfur flower, white Jupiter's beard, evening primroses, silver sage, and other gray-leafed plants.

related low-water perennials: Snow daisy (*Tanacetum niveum*) is a short-lived plant with aromatic gray-green divided foliage and clouds of tiny pure white daisies in dense panicles in late spring and early summer. Can self-sow prolifically in open, disturbed soil.

Tetraneuris scaposa (formerly *Hymenoxys scaposa*)

perky Sue, yellow plains daisy

grows 4–10 inches tall and 6–8 inches wide

best in zones 4–10

special attributes: Perky Sue is a small southwestern native with grassy mats of slender leaves. Cheerful yellow daisies appear on naked stems in early spring, winter in warm regions, and continue on and off till fall. Attracts butterflies. Self-sows mildly.

design ideas: Plant in the foreground or along paving. Combine with ice plants, plains skullcap, blue fescue, and blackfoot daisy. Nice with smaller cacti, yuccas, and agaves. Excellent roof garden plant.

related low-water perennials: Desert marigold (*Baileya multiradiata*), zones 7–10 in the West, is slightly larger yet compact, with cleft silver foliage and large golden daisies. This short-lived perennial blooms tirelessly, through winter in very mild climates and even in the hot desert summer if given a bit of moisture. Can be grown as an annual in cold, dry climates; resents humidity.

Teucrium cossonii var. *majoricum* (formerly *Teucrium majoricum*)

fruity germander

grows 4–6 inches tall and 12–24 inches wide

best in zones 7b–9, also zones 5b–6 in the West, resents humid heat

special attributes: Attractive low-growing mats of fruit-scented narrow gray foliage are topped in late spring and summer with heads of small rosy flowers, attracting bees. May rebloom in fall.

design ideas: Allow to drape over rocks or place in crevices between boulders. Plant where fragrant foliage can be touched. Lovely with 'Shimmer' evening primrose, 'Coronado' hyssop, prairie gayfeather, hop-flowered oregano, and purple mountain savory. Roof garden plant.

related low-water perennials: Creeping germander (*Teucrium chamaedrys* var. *prostrata*), zones 6–9, makes a 3-inch-tall ground cover with tiny evergreen leaves and underground stems. Small pink flowers appear in early summer.

Zauschneria californica

California fuchsia, hummingbird trumpet

grows 12–18 inches tall and wide

best in zones 5–10, resents humid heat

special attributes: A western native favored by hummingbirds, this plant opens tubular orange, red, and rarely white or peach blossoms on the tips of sprawling, fine-textured gray-green mounds for many weeks in the fall. Plants vary in height, leaf texture, and leaf color (light sage green to pure silver.) 'Wayne's Select' is almost white in leaf. Feeds caterpillars and adults of several species of sphinx moth.

design ideas: Combine with grasses, or with lavender, artemisia, Jerusalem sage, and santolina. Roof garden plant.

related low-water perennials: *Zauschneria garrettii* is the hardiest (zones 4b–5a) and earliest to bloom, starting in midsummer; best choice for regions with early frosts. 'Orange Carpet' is an extremely low-growing selection. *Zauschneria arizonica* is the largest at 2–3 feet; upright, late blooming, and aggressively spreading.

Ground Covers

Replacing a thirsty lawn with ground cover is an easy way to save water. These low-growing plants make living carpets of flowers and foliage and mingle well with larger plants of all kinds. They help create expansive, uncluttered visual spaces while often reducing maintenance. Many are proving themselves excellent roof garden plants as well. Criteria for this usage includes low water needs, long life, wind resistance, relatively low silhouette, attractive form, roots adapted to shallow soils with low fertility, and little if any need for regular cleanup.

    We indicate how fast these drought-resistant ground covers grow and note whether they spread aboveground or below, and we give recommended spacing for speedy coverage, telling you how far apart to plant them on center.

Antennaria parvifolia

dwarf pussytoes

spreads moderately aboveground, 3–6 inches tall, plant 8 inches apart on center

best in zones 3–7

special attributes: This extremely low-growing western native has fine-textured silver foliage that remains attractive year-round. Small cream-colored early-summer flowers in clusters on 3- to 6-inch stems go on to produce fluffy seed. More drought tolerant than commonly grown *Antennaria dioica*. Spent flower stalks should be removed to keep plant attractive. Withstands light foot traffic. Feeds caterpillars of painted lady and painted beauty butterflies. 'McClintock' has especially small foliage.

design ideas: Ideal between flagstones or beneath trees and shrubs that don't cast too deep a shade. Silver texture sets off yuccas well. Highly competitive roots exclude smaller perennials and other ground covers. Good for roof gardens.

related low-water ground covers: *Dymondia margaretae*, zones 8–10 on the West Coast, makes low gray mats with minute yellow daisies.

Callirhoe involucrata

wine cup, poppy mallow

spreads annually to 3–4 feet wide, 1 foot tall, plant 18 inches apart on center

best in zones 4–9 with hot summers

special attributes: This North American prairie native makes a wide wheel of lax stems growing from a single taproot. Wine-colored cupped flowers, often with white eyes, bloom all summer and fall. Paler pink and white forms exist. Bright green, lobed foliage cloaks the prostrate stems. Hardiness varies since it grows native over a wide climate range. Self-sows. Attracts bees. Larval food source for gray hairstreak butterfly.

design ideas: Mingle with verbenas, midsize grasses, datura, or sea lavender, or between yuccas, sotols, agaves, and small shrubs such as Russian sage, blue mist spirea, lavender, low-growing junipers, and artemisia. Also drapes nicely over walls and slopes.

related low-water ground covers: Pastel-colored *Callirhoe alceoides*, another North American wildflower, has more deeply cleft foliage.

Cerastium tomentosum

snow in summer

spreads quickly underground, 6–12 inches tall

best in zones 3–7

special attributes: The fine-textured silver foliage of this ground cover looks good for much of the year, especially if cut back by half after the bloom finishes. Masses of pure white flowers smother the plant in late spring for several weeks. Aggressive root system does not cohabit well with small perennials or bulbs.

design ideas: Combine with larger grasses such as Atlas fescue and Indian grass or with equally aggressive spreaders such as pink evening primrose. Mingle with artemisias, leadplant, Russian sage, and santolina for an easy-care silver chaparral-inspired planting. Plant between boulders for a frothy look. Good for roof gardens.

Ceratostigma plumbaginoides

leadwort, hardy plumbago

spreads slowly underground, 8–12 inches tall, plant 12 inches apart on center

best in zones 5–8, also zones 9–10 on the West Coast

special attributes: Fresh green midsize foliage emerges late in spring from leadwort's underground runners. In midsummer the first of a long succession of brilliant blue flowers open from ruddy calyces, drawing butterflies well into autumn. Fall foliage is deep red.

design ideas: Excellent companion to spring bulbs, as the late-emerging foliage allows the bulbs to mature their leaves and then masks them as they turn yellow and die down. Also beautiful with little bluestem. Grow under greedy-rooted trees with open canopies. Plant between shrubs that bloom late or have good fall foliage such as abelia, autumn sage, golden currant, and cutleaf smooth sumac. Roof garden plant.

Delosperma 'Kelaidis' (sold as Mesa Verde)

hardy peach ice plant

spreads quickly above ground to 2–3 inches tall, plant 12 inches apart on center

best in zones 5–7 in the West, also zones 8–10 on the West Coast, worth trying in zones 6–7 in the East

special attributes: Masses of iridescent peach-pink flowers completely hide the pale green succulent leaves of this ice plant in early summer. Blossoms repeat sporadically into the fall, attracting bees. Does not withstand foot traffic.

design ideas: Plant along sidewalks, on slopes, with yuccas, agaves, and cacti. Create a matrix with striped bearded iris or blue fescue. Excellent for roof gardens.

related low-water ground covers: *Delosperma* sp. 'Lesotho Pink' blooms with white-centered magenta flowers in late spring; *D. basuticum* has white or yellow flowers a bit earlier in spring. *Delosperma cooperi* (magenta), *D.* 'Lavender Ice' (lilac pink), and *D. dyeri* (red blend) are summer bloomers. *Delosperma nubigenum* bears yellow spring flowers and spreads the fastest of all; its leaves turn raspberry red in winter. All grow easily from cuttings.

Dichondra sericea

silver ponyfoot

spreads quickly aboveground, 1 inch tall, plant 12 inches apart on center

best in zones 8–10

special attributes: The small uniquely fan-shaped leaves are covered in silken hairs that give this South American plant a reflective, almost metallic sheen.

design ideas: Superb between architectural plants such as sotols, cycads, agaves, and yuccas in greens, grays, and blues, as well as with larger cacti. Trails nicely over walls and in containers, and softens harsh paving edges. Allow it to duke it out with purple heart, gopher spurge, and velvet creeper; overplant as a companion to rainlilies and ox-blood lilies. Good for roof gardens.

related low-water ground covers: Similar *Dichondra argentea* is often confused with this plant and is a southwestern native but not nearly as hearty a garden plant as *D. sericea*.

Lantana montevidensis (formerly *Lantana sellowiana*)

trailing lavender lantana

spreads quickly aboveground, 1–2 feet tall, plant 18 inches apart on center

best in zones 8–10

special attributes: This lax, low-growing lantana spreads prostrate stems covered in aromatic gray-green foliage. Lilac flower clusters appear at tips of branches, attracting butterflies. In hot climates heaviest bloom occurs from late summer through fall (and winter in mild areas). Leaves turn purplish in light-to-moderate frost, are deciduous in low 20s F. 'Trailing White' and 'White Lightning' are selections with white flowers; 'Lavender Swirl' is two-toned, opening white, gradually darkening lavender. 'Imperial Purple' has deeper purple flowers with white eyes.

design ideas: Plant as bank cover and for roof gardens, allow to weep over walls. Combine with stalwart architectural palms, large grasses, agaves, yuccas, and sotols.

related low-water ground covers: Plains native *Verbena canadensis* is a long-blooming heirloom perennial with cut foliage and flat heads of flowers that attract butterflies. Selections 'Annie' with lilac flowers and 'Miss Anne' with white blossoms are hardy in zones 4–8; heirloom hybrid 'Homestead Purple' is richer hued and hardy in zones 6–10. *Verbena peruviana* has red blossoms, zones 6b–10, and *V. tenera* 'Sissinghurst' has rosy pink flowers, zones 7–10.

Mahonia repens

creeping grapeholly

spreads slowly underground, 12–18 inches tall, plant 12 inches apart on center

best in zones 4–7, also 8–10 on the West Coast

special attributes: This western mountain native has leathery, hollylike foliage in bold whorls. It turns a muted burgundy in winter. Fragrant small yellow flowers attract bees in spring. These ripen to blue fruit, beloved of birds. One of the few plants that grow well in dry, deep shade.

design ideas: Ideal beneath trees and between large shrubs. Combine with common juniper and silver pussytoes for a simple, elegant, yet tough planting.

Paronychia kapela subsp. *serpyllifolia*

silver nailwort

spreads moderately aboveground, ¼ inch tall, plant 8 inches apart on center

best in zones 4–8, also zones 9–10 on the West Coast

special attributes: This thymelike spreader makes tidy but tough mats. The foliage turns peachy orange in cold weather. Tiny flowers are encased in papery white bracts that remain attractive for many weeks, giving the plant a pearly cast. Foliage is gray-green. Does not suffer from the winter desiccation, dieback, and disease problems that plague many thymes. Tolerates light foot traffic.

design ideas: One of the best plants for between flagstones. Serves as a friendly companion to small cacti as it remains low and its roots are not highly competitive. Very pretty with dollhouse yucca, early crocus, and snow iris. Good for roof gardens.

Phlox subulata

cushion phlox

spreads slowly aboveground, 3–10 inches tall, plant 12 inches apart on center

best in zones 4–8

special attributes: This North American native smothers itself in pink, white, rose, purple, crimson, or lavender flowers in spring for several weeks. Needlelike foliage forms dense mounds. In very sunny regions, foliage may burn in winter unless given some shade. Many selections are available.

design ideas: A favorite for early bloom in rock gardens. Also an ideal edge or fronting plant, or on slopes and for roof gardens. Mingle with Turkish veronica, ice plant, and sedum for a low tapestry planting. Lovely with dwarf bearded iris and Corsican pansy.

related low-water ground covers: *Phlox bifida* is not as dense or vigorous, better as an accent plant than a ground cover. It blooms white or lavender, with deeply cleft, snowflakelike flowers in spring.

Sedum sediforme

pale stonecrop

spreads moderately aboveground, 6–10 inches tall, plant 12 inches apart on center

best in zones 5b–10

special attributes: Pale stonecrop is a mat-forming succulent with plump blue-green leaves densely arranged on lax stems. Creamy flower clusters in early summer attract droves of bees. Propagates readily from cuttings.

design ideas: Plant as edging near sidewalks, on slopes, in roof gardens and rock gardens, as accent in crevices in stone walls and steps. Pretty with almost any small companion, especially those with red or orange flowers, such as California poppies and hummingbird trumpet.

related low-water ground covers: Blue spruce sedum (*Sedum* ×*luteolum*) is smaller, with yellow flowers and foliage that turns plum-tinted in winter. *Sedum rupestre* 'Angelina' has gold leaves tinged orange in winter.

Tanacetum densum subsp. *amani*

partridge feather

spreads slowly aboveground, 4–8 inches tall, plant 12 inches apart on center

best in zones 5–8, also zones 9–10 on the West Coast, dislikes humid heat

special attributes: The softly hairy, feather-shaped silver foliage of this plant is beautiful year-round. Sparse panicles of golden button-shaped flowers appear in early summer; they don't add much but don't detract either. Avoid overhead watering as the foliage can easily succumb to rot.

design ideas: Makes an excellent edge plant. Mingle with bold yuccas and small shrubs. Interplant in puzzle-shaped groupings with ice plants, sedums, and woolly veronica for a tapestry of evergreen ground covers with contrasting foliage textures and colors.

Tradescantia sillamontana

velvet creeper

spreads annually to 3 feet, 8–12 inches tall, plant 12 inches apart on center

best in zones 7–10

special attributes: The stems of this branched, sprawling succulent grow from a central tuft, carrying handsome oval gray-felted foliage. Rose pink flowers appear at stem tips in summer. Stems die back to resting rosettes in winter, renew growth in spring. Leaves become purplish in summer drought. Propagates easily from cuttings.

design ideas: Plant between stones of dry-stack walls or allow to spill from raised planters. Good for roof gardens with silver ponyfoot. Combine with cycads or sedges in dry shade. Nice with oxblood lilies, giant prairie lily.

related low-water ground covers: Purple heart (*Tradescantia pallida*, formerly *Setcreasea pallida*) has waxy purple, gray-green, or blue-green foliage, also excellent for roof gardens.

Veronica liwanensis

Turkish veronica

spreads moderately aboveground, ¼ inch tall, plant 8 inches apart on center

best in zones 4–8, also 9–10 on the West Coast

special attributes: This demure spreader makes mats of tiny, rounded, glossy rich green leaves, a lovely alternative to often scruffy and temperamental thymes. White-eyed blue flowers cover the plant in late spring for several weeks, giving the effect of pools of water and attracting bees. Tolerates light foot traffic.

design ideas: Ideal between paving stones or as a low-traffic lawn alternative. Creates a nice evergreen backdrop to the blossoms of early crocus, snow iris, and species tulips. Excellent for roof gardens.

related low-water ground covers: Woolly veronica (*Veronica pectinata*) is faster growing and slightly larger. Foliage is hairy and gray-green, taking on plum-lavender hues in winter. *Veronica oltensis* is the smallest, very slow growing, with tiny, lobed, shiny green foliage, ideal for rock gardens. Both are spring blooming, with sheets of blue flowers.

Grasses and Sedges

Grasses and sedges wave in the breeze and play with sunlight, bringing lively grace and texture to gardens and landscapes. We've noted which species are cool-season growers, best planted in early spring (fall in zones 7–10), and which are warm-season varieties, best planted in spring or summer (year-round in zones 7–10). For deciduous grasses or evergreen grasses and sedges damaged by winter cold, cut back before growth resumes.

Achnatherum calamagrostis

silver spike grass

grows 2–3 feet tall and wide

best in zones 4–8, also zones 9–10 on the West Coast, resents humid heat, cool-season grass

special attributes: This grass forms a graceful arching mound of medium-texture fresh green foliage. In midsummer, a bouquet of large glistening silvery flower plumes rises above the foliage, turning soft tan by late summer and persisting into fall and early winter. Very long lived, takes several years to reach maturity, gets better year after year. Good cut and dried flower.

design ideas: Ideal companion to larger perennials such as agastache, aromatic aster, and 'Lemon Queen' sunflower. Also mingles well with smaller shrubs such as leadplant, Russian sage, artemisia, blue mist spirea, and lavender.

Achnatherum hymenoides

Indian rice grass

grows 15–18 inches tall and wide

best in zones 3–9, resents humid heat, cool-season grass

special attributes: A western native with sparse foliage, Indian rice grass raises clouds of tiny flowers in airy panicles in early summer; these persist to create a lovely effect for months, continuing well into winter. Self-sows mildly.

design ideas: One of the best grasses to interplant with yuccas, agaves, and larger cacti. Also consorts well with penstemon, evening primrose, yellow onion, gaillardia, verbena, scarlet betony, and blue flax.

Bouteloua gracilis

blue grama

grows 6–15 inches tall and 12–18 inches wide

best in zones 3–8, resents humid heat, warm-season grass

special attributes: This widespread western native makes fine-textured hummocks of a soft gray-green. Turns tan in cold weather, greens up in midspring. Unique eyelashlike flowers expand in midsummer, held aloft on airy stems. These may vary from gray-green to charcoal gray to pale tan and almost yellow, and persist well into winter. A long-lived grass, it also self-seeds prodigiously. Best with limited mowing.

design ideas: Blue grama makes an excellent meadow grass or a casual low-traffic lawn. Leave broad spaces for perennials to thrive between the groupings of grass, as self-sown grass seedlings are hard to manage and will quickly crowd out perennials that are intermingled too tightly. Also pretty as an accent grass at the edge of paths or with yuccas and agaves. Roof garden plant.

related low-water grasses: 'Blonde Ambition' is a larger cultivar of blue gamma with pale chartreuse flowers that fade to soft yellow.

Buchloe dactyloides

buffalo grass

grows 3–6 inches tall with unlimited spread aboveground

best in zones 4–10 with hot summers, warm-season grass

special attributes: This shortgrass prairie native makes a dense, spreading turf of soft green. Some selections are more gray-green than others and vary in regional adaptability. Turns tan in cold weather, greens up in midspring. Male forms make attractive small flowers; female forms present a more uniform lawn. Needs no mowing and grows better with only one or two cuts a year. Spreads aggressively, so best with a physical barrier such as paving or edging between it and other plantings.

design ideas: Interplant with early small bulbs such as species tulips, crocuses, grape hyacinths, and snow iris to brighten the tawny dormant grass. Does not combine well with most smaller perennials or ground covers due to its aggressively spreading nature. Roof garden plant.

Carex eburnea

ivory sedge

grows 4–12 inches tall and 8–15 inches wide

best in zones 2–8

special attributes: Native to rocky limestone woodlands in the Northeast, Midwest, and Canada, this sedge thrives in dry shade. Narrow-leaved tussocks look like bright green trolls' hair. In autumn, the plant turns a soft butter yellow that glows in the shade. May self-sow lightly.

design ideas: Superb under trees where little else grows. Pretty in walls and between paving stones or mingled with larger hens and chicks in a lightly shaded rock garden. Combine with creeping grapeholly for textural contrast. Good roof garden plant.

related low-water sedges: Appalachian sedge (*Carex appalachica*) is very similar but more dependably evergreen and needs a bit more moisture to thrive.

Carex flacca

slender blue sedge

grows 4–8 inches tall with unlimited spread belowground

best in zones 4–8, also zones 9–10 on the West Coast

special attributes: The gracefully curved blue-gray foliage of this sedge forms loose tussocks. Flowers are insignificant. Self-seeds mildly.

design ideas: Makes a superb turf alternative in dry shade, beneath trees, for roof gardens, and in low-traffic areas. Also serves as a simple, serene-looking ground cover between midsize, open-branched shrubs such as western mock orange, golden currant, abelia, and boulder raspberry. Intermingle with velvet creeper.

Festuca 'Siskiyou Blue'

hybrid Idaho fescue

grows 10–15 inches tall and 15–18 inches wide

best in zones 4–8, also zones 9–10 on the West Coast, resents humid heat, cool-season grass

special attributes: This turquoise blue grass forms tussocks of fine, wiry foliage. Chartreuse flowers bloom in late spring and early summer, turning tawny later on. A hybrid between *Festuca glauca* (blue sheep's fescue, pictured together with 'Siskiyou Blue' in larger photo) and western native *F. idahoensis*, it is longer lived and less prolific at seeding than the former and bluer than the latter.

design ideas: Mingle in a meadow planting with gayfeather, wild petunia, and butterfly weed or plant as accents with evening primrose, striped iris, Spanish poppy, penstemons, yarrow, and hummingbird trumpet. Roof garden plant.

related low-water grasses: Gray-green *Festuca amethystina* is even more finely textured, with dark maroon flower stems and flowers, a prolific self-sower. Southwestern native *F. arizonica* tolerates more shade than the others and makes lovely hairlike pale green hummocks.

Festuca mairei

Atlas fescue

grows 2–3 feet tall and wide

best in zones 4–8, also zones 9–10 on the West Coast, resents humid heat, cool-season grass

special attributes: This khaki-green-and-buff grass looks like fireworks in the garden. The reflective foliage arches out like a fountain, with airy, persistent flower stalks adding to the lively demeanor. Its soft color yet arresting form help it blend well with almost any plant. Self-sows mildly when given extra moisture. Remains evergreen in mild climates.

design ideas: Beautiful with dramatic floral exclamation points of *Amaryllis bella-donna* or foxtail lily. Interweave with lavender, Russian sage, Apache plume, aromatic aster, or Jerusalem sage.

Koeleria macrantha

June grass

grows 10–18 inches tall and 6–12 inches wide

best in zones 3–7, also zones 8–10 on the West Coast, cool-season grass

special attributes: This widespread North American native has an upright habit and short gray-green to blue-green foliage. Pale flower plumes glisten in early summer, turn tawny later on, and persist well into winter. Self-sows mildly. Nice cut and dried flower.

design ideas: Mingle with wild petunia, prairie gayfeather, gaillardia, and butterfly weed in a prairie planting. Interplant with lipstick tulips. Place to backlight the glistening flowers. Roof garden plant.

related low-water grasses: Ruby grass (*Melinis nerviglumis*) is also

small but short lived, hardy to zone 6, tolerates humid heat. Foliage is blue-green and less upright, more fountainlike. Flower plumes are glittery, larger, and pink tinged when first opening. It can self-sow abundantly in moist situations.

'Autumn Glow' muhly grass

grows 3–5 feet tall and wide

best in zones 6b–10, warm-season grass

special attributes: This selection of the Texan native big muhly forms large tussocks of slender gray-green leaves. Creamy flower spikes are showy in autumn and dry to silver tones in winter. Nice cut flower. Typical *Muhlenbergia lindheimeri* has narrower vertical purplish gray plumes.

design ideas: Use as a repeated accent in naturalistic or meadow plantings. Good in narrow beds along sidewalks. Combine with aromatic aster, Maximilian sunflower, trailing lavender lantana, sunset hyssop, and autumn sage. Create a modern effect with rosemary, silver cenizas, large prickly pears, agaves, and yuccas.

related low-water grasses: *Muhlenbergia* ×*involuta* and 'Pink Flamingos', hybrids with *M. reverchonii* and *M. capillaris*, bear slender foliage and showy spikes of rosy flowers. Southwestern natives bull muhly (*M. emersleyi*), with purplish plumes, and deer muhly (*M. rigens*), with mounds of arching gray-green leaves and narrow tan spikes, are both hardy to zone 7. Bamboo muhly (*M. dumosa*), with shrubby stems covered in wispy fresh green foliage, prefers light shade and is hardy to zone 8.

Muhlenbergia reverchonii

autumn embers muhly

grows 15–18 inches tall and 18–24 inches wide

best in zones 5–10 with hot summers, warm-season grass

special attributes: This southern Great Plains native has fine-textured gray-green foliage in weeping mounds. Stunning airy panicles of ruddy red flowers expand like rosy clouds in autumn, then turn reddish brown and persist all winter.

design ideas: Deserves backlighting and consorts well with strongly architectural yuccas and agaves. Combine with aromatic aster, azure sage, leadwort, or hummingbird trumpet. Roof garden plant.

related low-water grasses: Popular Gulf muhly (*Muhlenbergia capillaris*) is slightly larger, earlier to bloom, and even brighter cerise red, with coarser and more upright foliage. It is hardy only to zone 6 and not as drought resistant. The selection 'Regal Mist' is more adaptable than the straight species.

Nassella tenuissima (formerly *Stipa tenuissima*)

Mexican feather grass

grows 15–18 inches tall and wide

best in zones 7–10, zones 5–6 in the West, can be grown as an annual grass in colder climates, cool-season grass

special attributes: This exceptionally fine-textured fresh green grass is native from South America up into the Southwest. Hairlike flowers and seeds make tawny fluff along the ends of arching stems. In cold winters or hot and dry summers, foliage turns blond; needs to be cut back before new growth emerges in spring (fall in hot climates). Self-sows prolifically. Short lived.

design ideas: Looks good with almost anything. Intersperse with yuccas, agaves, and large cacti. Create a matrix with scarlet gilia, oxblood lilies, or lavender.

related low-water grasses: European feather grass (*Stipa pennata*) is longer lived, with elegant elongated silvery seeds. It self-sows mildly and is a good substitute where Mexican feather grass proves invasive. Not as tolerant of humid heat.

Panicum virgatum

switch grass

grows 4–10 feet tall and 2–4 feet wide

best in zones 3–10, warm-season grass

special attributes: Switch grass is a widespread North American native with lush green to gray-blue foliage, some selections tinted red and with strong red fall color. Airy, loose flower panicles open in late summer and fall, and make a nice cut flower. Self-sows some. Many selections are available, varying in height, leaf color, and habit.

design ideas: Makes a strong accent plant; also useful as a part-season screen or hedge. Combine with Maximilian sunflower and aromatic aster to evoke the prairie. Bold and big enough to consort well with pines, junipers, and Arizona cypress. Lovely with the fall foliage colors of New Mexican olive, big tooth maple, and sumac. One of few low-water plants suited to rain gardens, as it enjoys inundation as well as drought.

Schizachyrium scoparium

little bluestem

grows 15–24 inches tall and 12–15 inches wide

best in zones 4–10, warm-season grass

special attributes: This widespread North American native offers green to gray-blue foliage that turns russet in fall on through winter, when its small flowers dry to silvery tufts. Self-sows some. Selections are regionally adapted: 'Prairie Blues' is a western seed strain more drought tolerant and upright than the eastern selection 'The Blues'.

design ideas: Combine with evening primrose and yarrow or place in sweeps with lavender or santolina, in front of sumac, intermingled with scarlet gilia and aromatic aster. Excellent meadow grass. Vertical habit complements modern designs.

related low-water grasses: North American native big bluestem (*Andropogon gerardii*) looks like a coarser, larger version of little bluestem, varies in foliage color from green to silvery blue, turns burgundy shades in autumn. Flower is a distinctive but not particularly showy three-forked panicle. Not quite as drought resistant as little bluestem.

Sorghastrum nutans

Indian grass

grows 5–7 feet tall and 2 feet wide

best in zones 4–10 with hot summers, warm-season grass

special attributes: Indian grass is a North American prairie native with green to silvery blue foliage. Tall yet rarely floppy. Large glistening bronzy plumes open in fall and persist into winter, cut and dry well. Birds relish the seed. 'Indian Steel' is extra blue and upright.

design ideas: Strikingly vertical and boldly elegant, Indian grass makes a strong statement paired with sumac, Maximilian sunflower, and Russian sage.

related low-water grasses: Hardy pampas grass (*Saccharum ravennae*) is not quite as drought resistant as Indian grass but is even larger, with stunning pale pink and then silvery plumes and coarser, gray-green foliage with sharp edges. It does not self-sow in the regions where true pampas grass (*Cortaderia sellowana*) is problematic.

Sporobolus wrightii

giant sacaton

grows 6–10 feet tall and 3–5 feet wide

best in zones 5–10 with hot summers, warm-season grass

special attributes: A large southwestern native, giant sacaton has coarse gray-green foliage. In late summer, tall, arching, tawny flowers shaped like fluffy fish-bones move with the slightest breeze, persist through fall. Some selections have flowers that are reddish before they dry. Salt-tolerant.

design ideas: Combine with trunking yuccas and large prickly pears, Maximilian sunflower, Apache plume, ceniza, groupings of leadplant, or large forms of rabbitbrush. Plant as a graceful hedge.

related low-water grasses: Western alkali sacaton (*Sporobolus airoides*) is half the size, with finer-textured gray-green foliage and airy clouds of rose-tinted tawny flowers in late summer and fall. Hardy in zones 4–10. Prairie dropseed (*S. heterolepis*) is a lovely fine-textured, shiny midsize grass with fragrant flowers and apricot fall color, not as drought tolerant as the western species, widely adapted, hardy in zones 3–8.

Zoysia 'Zeon'

hybrid Korean grass

grows 3 inches tall, spreading underground

best in zones 6–10, warm-season grass

special attributes: This low sod-forming grass features mossy-textured lush green foliage. Natural growth develops into mounds and humps. Remove thatch periodically if a more uniform, flat effect is desired. Remains evergreen into the mid-20s F.

design ideas: Aside from its use as a low-water lawn, plant between stepping-stones, as a small-scale ground cover, or for a mossy effect in Asian-inspired landscapes. Good roof garden plant.

related low-water grasses: 'Emerald' is a similar dwarf hybrid of *Zoysia tenuifolia* and *Z. japonica*. Mascarene grass (*Z. tenuifolia*) is especially low and fine textured, cold hardy to zone 8.

Bulbs, Corms, Tubers, and Rhizomes

The thrifty plants collectively called bulbs store food and water underground, dodging periods of extreme drought or cold by retreating below, then returning to grow and flower each year when conditions improve. They are usually bought and planted while dormant. Although many of the drought-resistant bulbs we list here are small or bloom for only a few weeks, they often appear in early spring or at other moments of the year when little else is blooming, an endearing and valuable habit. We've noted the sizes of individual bulb plants in our descriptions, but many varieties multiply to form large clumps over time. To achieve mature garden effects in new plantings, place these easy-care, often inexpensive plants in generous groups.

Allium flavum

yellow onion

grows 8–15 inches tall

best in zones 4–7, also zones 8–10 on the West Coast, resents humid heat

special attributes: Mopheads of yellow flowers rise like sparklers in mid to late summer from the yellow onion's sparse, grassy, blue-green foliage, attracting bees. Blooms when many gardens need a floral lift. Flowers last for well over a month. Self-sows mildly. Nice cut flower.

design ideas: Combine with small grasses. Thread between yuccas and agaves for looseness, floral exuberance, and spontaneity. Pretty with prairie petunia, compact pincushion flower, and hop-flowered oregano.

related low-water bulbs: *Allium carinatum* subsp. *pulchellum* is another easy-to-please mid-to-late-summer bloomer about twice the height and with larger but similarly loose and irregular flower heads in rosy purple or rarely white. It also self-sows if not deadheaded. Nice cut flower.

Anemone blanda

Grecian windflower

grows 4–6 inches tall

best in zones 5–8, also zones 9–10 on the West Coast, resents humid heat

special attributes: The daisylike white, blue, or pink flowers of Grecian windflower open in early spring on slender stems that bend in the wind, attracting bees; they close on cloudy or wet days. Foliage is dark green and divided into leaflets, unlike the grassy leaves of most bulbs. Goes summer dormant quickly after bloom. May self-sow profusely. Does not compete well in a grass matrix or a dense perennial planting. Soak dried tubers in water overnight before planting.

design ideas: Plant under deciduous trees and shrubs for early color. Combine with santolina and partridge feather, or Corsican pansy. Poke in among boulders or alongside stone steps.

related low-water bulbs: *Anemone coronaria* and *A.* x*fulgens* have poppy-like flowers on stems suitable for cutting, thrive in dry-summer regions of zones 8–10.

Crinum ×powellii

Cape lily

grows 3 feet tall

best in zones 6–10

special attributes:
The massive bulbs of this heirloom hybrid of *Crinum bulbispermum* and *C. moorei* push forth lush fountains of tapered green foliage, deciduous in winter after hard frost. Coarse stalks topped with large, fragrant pink or white trumpet-shaped flowers appear in late spring and repeat after rains. Blossoms open at dusk and attract sphinx moths. Excellent cut flower. Pink 'Cecil Houdyshel' is especially floriferous.

design ideas: Combine with abelia, artemisia, ceniza, or, for a more modern look, with switch grass. One of few low-water plants good for rain gardens where rain is harvested and soil alternates between dry and waterlogged.

related low-water bulbs: *Crinum macowanii* (zones 8–10) bears fragrant pink-striped flowers. Belladonna lily (*Amaryllis belladonna*), zones 9–10, requires dry summers, bears fragrant pink or more rarely white trumpets on bare stems after fall rains; its hybrid ×*Amarcrinum* 'Fred Howard' has scented pink flowers in summer, widely adapted in zones 7–10.

Crocus chrysanthus

snow crocus

grows 3–4 inches tall

best in zones 4–8, resents humid heat

special attributes: Snow crocus forms ever-larger clumps and self-seeds to make great colonies. Bees adore the late winter and early spring flowers. Cup-shaped blossoms come in white, pale lavender, purple, yellow, and bicolored forms. Short, grassy foliage emerges with the flowers, going dormant before summer. Rodents relish the corms, and birds may occasionally shred flower petals in misguided courtship rituals and rivalries.

design ideas: Lovely in a buffalo grass lawn or cactus garden for early color. Looks wonderful growing through ice plant, thyme, or Turkish veronica foliage.

related low-water bulbs: Gold bunch crocus (*Crocus ancyrensis*) is smaller and even earlier blooming, with egg-yolk yellow flowers. Fragrant lavender goblets of *C. goulimyi* appear just before its leaves emerge in fall; hardy in zones 7–10 (and zone 6 in the West). In light shade and more temperate, humid climates, lavender or white fall-blooming *C. speciosus* (zones 5–7) and spring-flowering *C. vernus* and *C. tommasinianus* are well adapted. The latter is more rodent resistant than most crocus species.

Eremurus hybrids

foxtail lily

grows 3–8 feet tall

best in zones 5–9, resents humid heat

special attributes:
Striking 1- to 2-foot spikes of flowers in yellow, white, orange, pink, and peach, beloved of bees, rise on the tall, sturdy naked stems of foxtail lily in late spring and early summer, lasting for several weeks. Rosettes of strap-shaped blue-gray foliage die down later in summer. Excellent cut flower. Self-sows some. Dislikes competition; give room for sun to reach foliage during its brief appearance.

design ideas: Plant with larger grasses, midsize shrubs such as Apache plume, joint fir, or rabbitbrush, and bold trunk-forming yuccas.

related low-water bulbs: *Eremurus stenophyllus* (formerly *E. bungei*) is the shortest, at 2–4 feet, with yellow flowers. *Eremurus robustus*, peachy pink, and *E. himalaicus*, white, are statuesque at 6–10 feet. Sea squill (*Urginea maritima*), dry summer regions of zones 8b–10, forms massive bulbs with lush, wavy green rosettes of winter foliage. Leafless 4- to 6-foot spikes of white flowers appear after fall rains.

Gladiolus communis subsp. *byzantinus* 'Cruentus'

corn flag

grows 18–24 inches tall

best in zones 6–9, also zone 10 on the West Coast, worth trying in zone 5b in the West

special attributes: This heirloom plant makes corms that send up flattened, spear-shaped leaves in early to late winter. Showy spikes of magenta flowers top foliage mid to late spring, attracting bees, bumblebees, and hummingbirds. 'Albus' has white flowers and is slightly smaller all around. Foliage dies down by midsummer. Seedlike cormels multiply near original corm, mature to flowering size after three years. Good cut flower.

design ideas: Combine with snow daisy and artemisia. Mingle with feather grass in meadow-inspired plantings.

related low-water bulbs: *Gladiolus communis* subsp. *communis* (often sold as *G. byzantinus*) and *G. italicus* (both zones 5–10) reach 1 foot and produce much smaller magenta blossoms, narrow bluish leaves.

Iris germanica hybrids

bearded iris

grows 6–36 inches tall

best in zones 4–7, also zones 8–10 on the West Coast, fewer disease and insect problems in regions with low humidity

special attributes: Ever popular bearded iris offer brief but breathtaking late-spring flowers in all colors, often fragrant. Attractive to bees. Swordlike foliage adds interest, goes dormant in cold winters. Dividing, renovating, and replanting rhizomes every five years maintains vigor and bountiful bloom. Good cut flower.

design ideas: A quintessential cottage garden plant—combine with Cheyenne mock orange, taller penstemons, catmint, dianthus, California poppies, and love-in-a-mist. For a more modern look, blend with feather grass or Atlas fescue.

related low-water bulbs: Dwarf bearded iris (*Iris pumila* hybrids) bloom a month earlier, are only 6–12 inches tall. *Iris pallida*, with fragrant lavender flowers, is best known for the stunning yellow- and white-striped foliage variants 'Aurea Variegata' and 'Argentea Variegata'. Heirloom white flag (*I. albicans*) comes in white and pale blue forms and is the best bearded iris for hot climates.

Iris reticulata

snow iris

grows 4–8 inches tall

best in zones 4–8, also zones 9–10 on the West Coast, resents humid heat

special attributes: The large blue, indigo, cream, or purple flowers of this iris emerge in late winter and early spring, followed by sparse, grassy foliage. The leaves die down within two months. Flowers are honey scented and attract bees on warm, sunny days. Bulbs clump up to form dense bouquets of flowers in a few years.

design ideas: Ideal interplanted in buffalo grass for early color. Nice with snow crocus nestled among hens and chicks or amid smaller cacti. Plant into evergreen ground covers such as nailwort, thyme, ice plant, or Turkish veronica.

related low-water bulbs: Deep blue *Iris histrioides* is closely related and one parent of many of the so-called reticulata hybrids. 'Frank Elder' and 'Katharine Hodgkin' are hybrids in smoky teal hues that have proven more tolerant of heavy clay soils.

Iris xiphium and hybrids

Spanish iris

grows 10–18 inches tall

best in zones 6–8, also zones 9–10 on the West Coast, worth trying in zone 5 in the West

special attributes: This is a slender-leafed bulbous iris with elegant blue and white flowers in the wild species, and yellow, bronze and bicolored flowers in the hybrids. Narrow leaves emerge in fall (spring in colder climates), die down after bloom. Flowers appear early to late spring, depending on variety. Excellent cut flower.

design ideas: Combine with artemisia or silver germander, or mass as a seasonal floral contrast to large succulents, yuccas, and shrub palms.

related low-water bulbs: *Iris xiphium* var. *filifolia* has attractive grassy leaves; *I. xiphium* var. *lusitanica* blooms yellow. *Iris tingitana* has dark blue flowers, leaves with a metallic silver sheen. Dutch irises (*I.* ×*hollandica*) are larger, leafier hybrids of Spanish iris that are not all as drought tolerant. A few selections such as 'Blue Magic' and 'Wedgewood' are reliably waterwise.

Muscari species

grape hyacinth

grows 4–10 inches tall

best in zones 4–8, depending on selection; also zones 9–10 on the West Coast

special attributes: Clusters of fragrant urn-shaped blue, white, rarely pink or pale yellow single or double flowers grace grape hyacinth for several weeks in late winter and early spring, attracting bees. Grassy bright green foliage of some species comes up in fall, while others' leaves emerge along with spring bloom. Foliage of most grape hyacinths goes summer dormant in all but the mildest climates. *Muscari armeniacum* and, in warmer climates, *M. neglectum* are heirlooms with deep blue flowers, self-sow prolifically. *Muscari botryoides*, *M. aucheri*, and their hybrids are better where masses are not wanted. 'Blue Magic' (pictured) and sterile 'Saffier' are extra-long-blooming selections.

design ideas: Plant beneath deciduous trees and shrubs, in a buffalo grass lawn. Nice with species tulips, silver pussytoes or ponyfoot, dwarf sedums, and cushion phlox.

related low-water bulbs: Muscari-like *Bellevalia pycnantha* sends up fragrant blue-black flower spikes amid waxy blue-green foliage.

Narcissus tazetta 'Grand Primo'

'Grand Primo' daffodil

grows 18–30 inches tall

best in zones 6b–10

special attributes:
This cluster-flowered heirloom sends up fans of straplike matte green leaves in late fall to early winter. Fragrant flowers follow in early spring, their white petals and pale yellow cups showing up well against the lush foliage. Leaves fade in May. Similar or identical bulbs are sold as 'Scilly White' or 'White Pearl'. Good cut flower.

design ideas: Intermingle with artemisia, rosemary, and silver germander. Grow through blue sedge. Combine with cycads and yuccas for a modern look.

related low-water bulbs: *Narcissus* 'Erlicheer' has clusters of double, very fragrant ivory flowers. 'Avalanche' carries clustered single white flowers with yellow cups. Paperwhites

(*N. papyraceus*), Chinese sacred lilies (*N. tazetta* subsp. *lacticolor*), and *N. italicus*, zones 8b–10, grow and flower in winter; they need frequent division to allow bulbs to size up and bloom, so are higher maintenance.

Rhodophiala bifida (formerly *Hippeastrum advenum*)

oxblood lily

grows 10–15 inches tall

best in zones 7b–10

special attributes: This dwarf heirloom amaryllis grows in clumps with clusters of deep red flowers on slender stems following late summer or fall rains. Pliant, narrow shining green leaves emerge after bloom from long-necked bulbs, persist through winter, yellow off and die down in late spring.

design ideas: Mass with velvet creeper or silver ponyfoot. Under deciduous trees, combine with blue sedge. Dramatic seasonal color accent with smaller yuccas and agaves.

related low-water bulbs: *Rhodophiala bifida* var. *spathacea* produces pink flowers and is less vigorous.

Sternbergia lutea

autumn daffodil

grows 6–8 inches tall

best in zones 6–8, also zones 9–10 on the West Coast, worth trying in zone 5b in the West

special attributes: This fall-flowering heirloom bulb opens waxy golden flowers like giant crocuses after autumnal rains, just as or before grasslike foliage emerges. Leaves are glossy, persist through winter and fade in late spring. Attracts bees.

design ideas: Edge or foreground accent. Combine with pale stonecrop and leadwort. Nest between boulders on slopes.

Tulipa batalinii

dwarf species tulip

grows 4–8 inches tall

best in zones 4–7, resents humid heat, needs cold winters

special attributes: This dwarf species tulip forms dense bouquets after a few years. Soft yellow, apricot, or red flowers are rounded, longer lasting, and more tulip-like than those of most dwarf species. Bees relish the lightly fragrant flowers for several weeks in spring. Attractive wavy-edged blue-green foliage coincides with emerging flowers, dies down soon after bloom.

design ideas: Excellent in buffalo grass lawns. Combine with grape hyacinth, Corsican pansy, woolly veronica, sedum, and ice plant, or nestle among smaller yuccas and cacti.

related low-water bulbs: *Tulipa humilis* is slightly smaller, earlier blooming, with narrow green foliage and pink, magenta, or white star-shaped flowers. *Tulipa linifolia* and *T. maximowiczii* are virtually indistinguishable, with narrow gray-green foliage and red flowers. All persist and increase dependably, unlike the larger hybrids.

Tulipa clusiana var. *chrysantha*

Persian tulip

grows 8–12 inches tall

best in zones 5b–8, also zones 9–10 on the West Coast

special attributes: This heirloom tulip sends up gray leaves and golden flowers flamed red on outer petals in midspring. Flowers close at night and on cloudy or windy days. Flexible stems bend to track the sun. One of the few tulips that thrives in hot climates. Attracts bees. Foliage dies down soon after bloom. 'Tubergen's Gem' is shorter, similarly vibrant. Taller *Tulipa clusiana* var. *clusiana* has red-and-white blossoms blotched purple in the center; other selections include white-and-rose 'Lady Jane', pale-yellow-and-rose 'Tinka' and 'Cynthia'.

design ideas: Combine with June grass in meadow gardens, or with mountain basket of gold, cushion phlox, and woolly veronica in rock gardens. Mingle with smaller succulents. In mild climates, plant in large groups with bluebonnets (*Lupinus texensis*) or California poppies.

related low-water bulbs: Large-flowered, lilac pink *Tulipa bakeri*, taller burnt orange *T. orphanidea*, and scarlet *T. praecox* all thrive in both warm- and cold-winter climates, are humidity tolerant.

Tulipa kaufmanniana

species tulip

grows 6–12 inches tall

best in zones 4–8, resents humid heat, needs cold winters

special attributes: This compact, very early tulip sends up surprisingly big flowers, red or rose outside and white, cream, or yellow inside. Flowers close on cloudy days and open wide in warm sunlight, attracting bees. Foliage is bulky and gray-green, often with interesting maroon striations or spots; emerges with flowers and dies down soon after they finish.

design ideas: Best planted between emergent perennials and ground covers such as leadwort to help hide large leaves as they go dormant. Lovely with partridge feather or silver sage.

related low-water bulbs: *Tulipa greigii* has large rose or red flowers, foliage is even more strongly mottled. Slightly smaller and a bit later to bloom, *T. vvedenskyii* has jaunty, flame-shaped orange-red flowers and handsome wavy-edged blue-green foliage; may self-sow.

Zephyranthes drummondii (formerly *Cooperia pedunculata*)

giant prairie lily, rain lily

grows 8 inches tall

best in zones 7–10

special attributes: This southwestern native bulb has sparse, fleshy gray-green leaves that persist year-round except in severe drought. Cup-shaped white flowers open at dusk after rains from March to June (or into fall in dry years). Flowers are sweet scented and attract sphinx moths and hummingbirds.

design ideas: Plant generous groups into informal lawns and on embankments. Add as seasonal accents to rock gardens or with yuccas and agaves. Combine with velvet creeper, pale stonecrop, and ghost plant.

related low-water bulbs: *Zephyranthes chlorosolen* (formerly *Cooperia drummondii*) is smaller, with slender leaves, and flowers after rains from June to November. *Zephyranthes* sp. La Buffa Rosa strain (pink to white or bicolored) and *Z.* sp. 'Cookie Cutter Moon' (white) rapidly form clumps, bloom mid to late summer, grow leaves in fall and winter.

Vines

Like trees, vines help green up and soften spaces by shading walls,
fences, and—when trained over arbors—people. Vines climb in
different ways; some stick directly to a surface, while others need
to wrap around or twine. To get twining vines up a wall, post, or
other surface, provide a taut wire or cable fastened top and bottom
and secured or threaded through eyelets, or attach wire mesh to a
fence or around a pole.

Bignonia capreolata 'Tangerine Beauty'

orange crossvine

grows to 15–30 feet or more

best in zones 6–10

special attributes:
This is a floriferous heirloom selection of a native eastern North American vine. Stems carry a dense cover of pointed leaves and climb readily by means of short tendrils. Showy trumpet-shaped coral-orange flowers with yellow throats smother vines in spring and repeat this mass bloom four to five times through growing season, attracting humming-birds and bees. More tolerant of drought and alkaline soils than other *B. capreolata* selections. Thickened rootstocks send out trailing stems (runners) that may layer and spread unless restrained. Introduced by author from old gardens of central Texas.

design ideas: Train on arbors for shade; as topiary cone or pyramid. Plant to drape over and soften walls and ledges. Climbs rough masonry or fencing without support. Combine with passionflower or Lady Banks' rose.

Campsis radicans

trumpet creeper

grows to 15–30 feet or more

best in zones 5–9

special attributes:
This showy native of eastern North America puts out rampant climbing stems that attach directly to wood or masonry. These carry lush green foliage and summer trusses of large tubular orange, red, or amber-yellow blossoms, attractive to bees and hummingbirds. Suckering stems can be controlled with root barriers to limit spread.

design ideas: Train up a tall post, thick arbor, or fence; makes an attractive cover for an old tree stump.

related low-water vines: Chinese trumpet creeper (*Campsis grandiflora*) and hybrids with *C. radicans*, *C. ×tagliabuana* 'Madame Galen' and 'Indian Summer', are soft orange cultivars hardy in zones 6–10, larger flowered and less rampant than *C. radicans*.

Clematis texensis

scarlet leather flower

grows to 10–15 feet

best in zones 5–10

special attributes:
This Texas native bears urn-shaped bright red flowers, creamy yellow to red inside. These continue to open all summer and into fall, attracting hummingbirds and bumblebees. Leathery gray-green leaves with pliant petioles grasp twigs of adjacent plants, supports. Glistening starburstlike seed clusters. In humid climates, foliage sometimes shows harmless mildew. May turn yellow in fall. Dies down to perennial roots each winter, unlike most vines.

design ideas: Small-scale vine to climb picket fence, trellis, mailbox post. Good on porch post to watch hummingbirds up close. Combine with silver dollar vine.

related low-water vines: Southeastern *Clematis glaucophylla* shows its warm pink flowers against gray-blue leaves, while *C. pitcheri* combines green foliage with purple blossoms attractive to bumblebees. *Clematis texensis* hybrids 'Gravetye Beauty', 'Duchess of Albany', and 'Princess Diana' carry red to pink bell-shaped flowers and are not nearly as drought resistant as the species.

Lonicera reticulata 'Kintzley's Ghost'

silver dollar vine, moon vine

grows to 15 feet

best in zones 4–8

special attributes: Midwestern and northeastern native silver dollar vine bears rounded waxy blue-green foliage. The leaves at the tips of stems turn silver as summer progresses, shimmering all over the vine until hard frost. Small yellow flowers, encircled by leaves, bloom in late spring and attract bees. Needs thin supports to twine on to climb, such as wire, smaller branches of trees and large shrubs, or thin wooden lattice.

design ideas: A lovely, well-behaved vine for arbors and fences. The pale green foliage and "silver dollars" shine in light shade and in evening gardens. In full sun, combine with similarly well-mannered red-flowered *Clematis texensis* for a companionable vining duo.

Lonicera sempervirens

coral honeysuckle vine

grows to 10 feet

best in zones 4–10, varies with selection

special attributes: This eastern North American native has thick blue-green foliage on twining stems. In cold climates where it is not evergreen, it is still one of the last to lose its leaves and first to re-emerge in spring. In late spring and sporadically for most of the growing season, clusters of orange, red, or sometimes yellow tubular flowers attract hummingbirds in droves. Feeds caterpillars of the clearwing sphinx moth.

design ideas: Lovely on arbors and trellises near windows where the steady parade of hummingbirds can be watched. Can be safely let loose on trees without fear of rampant smothering.

Parthenocissus quinquefolia 'Engelmannii'

Virginia creeper, woodbine

grows to 15–30 feet or more

best in zones 3–10

special attributes: Virginia creeper is a leafy vine native to much of North America that climbs rough surfaces with small branched clinging tendrils. Tiny insignificant flowers attract bees before ripening to blue-purple berries that birds like to eat. The five-parted foliage turns brilliant burgundy to orange-red in fall. Feeds caterpillars of many sphinx moth species. 'Engelmannii' has tidier foliage than the species and is less rampant.

design ideas: Creates dense cover for masonry walls and fast shade for arbors. Can be allowed to trail over ledges and boulders. A vine-covered backdrop makes a brilliant fall statement with silvery blue limber pine and Arizona cypress or dark green 'Taylor' juniper.

related low-water vines: 'Hacienda Creeper', zones 7–10, is a small-leafed selection from northeastern Mexico with bronze

new growth and glossy summer foliage turning red in late fall. Seven-leaf creeper (*P. heptaphylla*), zones 6–10, of central Texas makes a dwarf scrambling vine.

Passiflora caerulea

blue passion flower

grows to 15–30 feet or more

best in zones 7–10

special attributes: This vine's leathery five-lobed leaves are evergreen to the low 20s F. Climbing rapidly by tendrils, it creates a lush backdrop for intricate blue-and-cream summer flowers attractive to bees. Rings at center of flower are deep blue in typical form, light blue in 'Clear Sky', cream in 'Constance Eliot'. Edible showy orange fruits. Feeds caterpillars of heliconia and Julia butterflies, several fritillary species.

design ideas: Use as privacy cover for iron fencing. Plant up close where blossoms' intricacy can be appreciated. Combine with 'Tangerine Beauty' crossvine.

related low-water vines: Maypop (*Passiflora incarnata*), a native of eastern North America with lacy blue flowers, and its purple hybrid 'Incense' are both aggressive spreaders, zones 6–10. 'Lavender Lady' and pure white 'Quasar' are hybrids of *P. caerulea*; soft blue southwestern native *corona de Christi* (*P. foetida*) is the most drought resistant, zones 8–10.

Rosa banksiae 'Lutea'

Lady Banks' rose

grows to 15–30 feet or more

best in zones 6–10

special attributes: This vigorous climbing or sprawling rose creates large mounding or layered bushes when untrained. Long canes are covered in glossy green three-parted foliage, have few or no thorns. Clusters of double creamy yellow flowers smother plants in early spring, drawing bees.

design ideas: Train on arbors for shade, plant to drape over and soften large masonry walls and ledges. Use as hedge or barrier planting or on an embankment. Can be sheared right after bloom. Combine with scarlet leather flower or coral honeysuckle to extend floral interest.

related low-water vines: White Lady Banks' rose (*Rosa banksiae* 'Alba Plena') bears clusters of double white flowers lightly scented of violets.

Vitis vinifera

grape

grows to 15–25 feet or more

best in zones 6–10

special attributes: This vigorous vine, densely furnished with handsome scalloped leaves, climbs by small tendrils. Tiny, inconspicuous, fragrant green flowers, relished by bees, open in early summer and ripen to clusters of green, red, or purple fruit in late summer or fall, used for the table, juice, wine, and jelly. Birds and raccoons also relish the fruit. Good yellow or red fall foliage. Prune annually for best production. Many cultivars; 'Black Monukka', 'Flame', and 'Thompson' are seedless. Feeds caterpillars of several sphinx moth species.

design ideas: Provide a wired trellis or post to climb; allow to cover arbor and provide shade.

related low-water vines: Seedless hybrids with North American grape species, hardy in zones 5–8, include 'Somerset Seedless', 'Trollhagen', 'Himrod', 'Vanessa', and 'Reliance'. Seedless varieties hardy in zones 7–10 include 'Venus', 'Orlando', 'Centennial', and 'Seibel 9110'.

Annuals, Biennials, and Short-Lived Perennials

These short-lived flowering plants can either be planted as small seedlings or sown directly into the garden. After flowering, the plants featured here self-sow and return in following seasons, helping fill bare spaces between other plants and lending floral spontaneity to gardens and landscapes. Plants indicated as warm-season growers should be planted after the last frost to grow through summer. Cool-season growers, also known as hardy annuals, sprout and grow best in fall or spring, or in the winter in very mild climates. They flower in winter or spring in warm winter regions, and in summer in climates with cold winters. In cold climates these can be sown directly into the ground in fall or planted in early spring. In zones 7–10 they should be sown or planted in the fall.

Antirrhinum majus

snapdragon

grows 12–24 inches tall and 12–18 inches wide

best in all zones, cool-season annual in coldest and hottest climates, biennial or short-lived perennial in moderate climates, winter hardy to zone 5

special attributes: With a bushy, branching habit and bright green foliage, snapdragons are loved for their large, snout-shaped flowers in all colors but blue; they bloom for months. Squeeze blossoms at the base to make them move like talking mouths. Deadheading encourages longer bloom. Self-sows moderately. Excellent cut flower. Bee and bumblebee plant; feeds caterpillars of the buckeye butterfly.

design ideas: Mix this classic cottage garden plant with other self-sowers such as poppies, blue flax, snow daisy, larkspur, and love-in-a-mist. Lends seasonal floral color to textural yuccas and smaller grasses.

related low-water plants: Perennial *Antirrhinum braun-blanquetii* has narrower leaves and soft yellow flowers; hybridizes readily with *A. majus*, often producing nice color blends and dependably perennial plants.

Consolida ajacis (formerly *Consolida ambigua*)

larkspur

grows 2–4 feet tall and 12–18 inches wide

best in all zones, cool-season annual

special attributes: Larkspur has sparse, feathery foliage and deep blue, pink, pale blue, or white flowers in racemes on lanky upright stems for many weeks. Self-sows with abandon. One of the best plants for butterflies, also attracts bees and bumblebees. Flowers cut and dry well, especially double-flowered selections.

design ideas: Lovely with orange poppies, gaillardia, yarrow, red standing cypress, and butterfly weed. Slender upright habit allows it to slip easily into plantings, loosening compositions while adding notes of bright color.

related low-water plants: Cloud larkspur (*Consolida regalis*) is a smaller, many-branched plant that makes an airy display of flowers in blue or white, rarely pink.

Erigeron divergens

cloud daisy

grows 6–12 inches tall and 12–18 inches wide

best in all zones, biennial or cool-season annual

special attributes: This dainty western native has lobed leaves in small, flat rosettes, growing into sparse, airy mounds topped with myriad nodding buds that open to up-facing white daisies, sometimes tinged lilac. Flowers partially close at night, open in sun, stay in bloom for months, attracting small native bees. Self-sows prolifically.

design ideas: Naturalize in gravel, with short grasses, and among larger yuccas, agaves, sotols, and cacti.

related low-water plants: Santa Barbara daisy (*Erigeron karvinskianus*) is a short-lived perennial native to Mexico. It makes an evergreen ground cover in zones 8–10 and is often planted as a cascading annual elsewhere, 1 foot tall, 2–4 feet wide. Daisies are white with pink reverses.

Eschscholzia californica

California poppy

grows 10–15 inches tall and 12–18 inches wide

best in all zones, cool-season annual in zone 5 and colder, biennial or short-lived perennial in moderate climates, resents humid heat

special attributes: This western native offers large, satiny four-petaled flowers, typically orange but also red, cream, pale yellow, pink, and semidouble. Blooms for months if not too hot, attracting bees; closes on cloudy, windy, and rainy days. Beautiful blue-gray, finely dissected foliage. Self-sows tremendously. Resents crowding.

design ideas: Lovely among small grasses, yuccas, sotols, and agaves. Combine with desert bluebell, blue flax, evening primrose, penstemon, plains skullcap, lavender, and silver artemisia.

related low-water plants: Smaller North American poppies include orange or yellow southwestern *Eschscholzia mexicana* and petite pale yellow *E. caespitosa*, which grows in chaparral along the Pacific coast and resents heat of any kind. Tulip poppy, *Hunnemannia fumariifolia*, more upright and with larger golden flowers, is the most heat and humidity tolerant species.

Euphorbia marginata

snow on the mountain

grows 2–4 feet tall

best in all zones, warm-season annual

special attributes: This Great Plains native has stout, downy stems that branch in threes and carry oval gray-green leaves, with larger white-margined bracts at the tips of the stems. Small true flowers at center attract butterflies, bees. Effect is like a small white poinsettia, in color from late summer until frost. Exudes white sap when bruised or cut; three-sided seed capsules explode when ripe. Self-sows mildly.

design ideas: Thread through cottage and meadow gardens; mingle with aromatic aster and Maximilian sunflower.

related low-water plants: Southern Great Plains native snow on the prairie (*Euphorbia bicolor*) has narrower bracts. Wild poinsettia (*E. cyathophora*) makes bushy 1- to 2-foot plants with green leaves and irregular pointed bracts splashed red at the base; 'Yokoi's White' is variegated.

Gaillardia pulchella

Indian blanket, firewheel

grows 10–24 inches tall and 6–18 inches wide

best in all zones, cool-season annual

special attributes: This roadside wildflower, native to the south-central prairies of North America, carries festively colored daisies from late spring to early summer and into fall in cooler climates. Blossoms appear on rough stems cloaked in coarse, hairy green foliage rising from leafy rosettes, Typical flowers have rusty orange rays with yellow tips around reddish centers. Variants on sandy soils may be entirely orange-red. Self-sows abundantly. Attracts butterflies and bees, feeds caterpillars of the bordered patch butterfly.

design ideas: Mingle with small grasses or combine with blue sage, larkspur, blue flax, and giant prairie lily.

related low-water plants: Nurseries offer double-flowered pom-pom strains in yellow, red, wine, and orange.

Glaucium corniculatum

horned poppy

grows 15–18 inches tall and wide

best in zones 4–7, also zones 8–10 on the West Coast, biennial or short-lived perennial

special attributes: Horned poppy is a handsome, wild-looking plant with strong texture. The stunning scalloped blue-gray foliage grows in evergreen rosettes. These give rise to orange or amber poppylike flowers the second year, followed by unusual long, thin, curved seedpods that look like horns. Blooms for months in late spring and summer. Self-sows mildly. Attractive to bees.

design ideas: Mingle with grasses, larkspur, blue penstemons, blue flax, verbena, blue sage, and evening primrose.

related low-water plants: *Glaucium flavum* is a larger 2- to 3-foot plant with amber flowers. *Glaucium grandiflorum* has bigger orange-red flowers and foliage that is not as blue or scalloped. Diminutive *G. squamigerum* has apricot-colored flowers and stays under a foot in height. Biennial Armenian poppy (*Papaver triniifolium*) has smaller, lacier blue foliage rosettes and many smaller apricot flowers on a branched 18-inch stem.

Ipomoea sloteri (formerly *Quamoclit ×multifida*)

cardinal climber

grows to 15–20 feet

best in all zones, warm-season annual

special attributes: This fast-growing twining vine has slender stems that carry deeply lobed green leaves. Bright red tubular flowers bloom all summer, attracting hummingbirds. Self-sows mildly.

design ideas: Makes a lush cover for wire fencing and topiary cones or pyramids. Combine with passion flower.

related low-water plants: Cypress vine (*Ipomoea quamoclit*) makes feathery pale green foliage as a backdrop for charming red or white tubular flowers.

Ipomopsis rubra (formerly *Gilia rubra*)

standing cypress, skyrocket

grows 3–6 feet tall and 1 foot wide

best in zones 4–9, also zone 10 on the West Coast, biennial

special attributes: This central and eastern North American native starts life as a humble feathery foliage rosette. The second year a tall, dramatic flower spike shoots up, covered in tubular flowers beloved of hummingbirds. The blossoms are typically orange-red but sometimes peach or yellow. Blooms for two months or more in summer and fall. Self-sows mildly. Resents crowding.

design ideas: Mingle with bull muhly, alkali sacaton, and Atlas fescue. Plant amid yuccas, sotols, and agaves for feathery but bold exclamation points of color. Dramatic on steep slopes.

related low-water plants: Western native *Ipomopsis aggregata* forms a shorter, branched plant with red, pink, peach, or white flowers. Several smaller relatives, native southwestern *Gilia* species, have purple, lavender, or white flowers that open in late afternoon.

Nigella damascena

love-in-a-mist

grows 12–18 inches tall and 6–12 inches wide

best in all zones, cool-season annual

special attributes: The feathery light green foliage of love-in-a-mist sets off starry blue, purple, mauve, or white flowers encased in similarly feathery bracts, giving the plant a frothy look. Blooms for many weeks. Large, attractive, balloonlike papery seedpods with maroon stripes ripen to tan. Needs little space and comes up easily between plants. Self-sows profusely. Excellent for cutting and drying, seedpods also.

design ideas: Good at the edge of paths. Mingle with bearded iris to soften their spiky demeanor. Combine with California poppy, Mexican feather grass, penstemons, dianthus, and silver sage.

related low-water plants: *Nigella hispanica* is sparser, with darker blue, indigo, or white flowers. It tolerates more heat so begins bloom later and continues on into the hot season.

Papaver rhoeas

corn poppy

grows 6–20 inches tall and 6–12 inches wide

best in all zones, cool-season annual

special attributes: This hairy, tap-rooted annual has irregular lobed leaves. Showy red four- to six-petaled flowers with a boss of dark stamens and black markings in the center appear for several weeks in spring or early summer, attract bees, and ripen small barrel-shaped seed capsules. Self-sows abundantly. Seed strains with pastel and double flowers in shades of pink, lilac, white, and red are available.

design ideas: Overplant as companion for spring bulbs; combine with larkspur, love-in-a-mist, and small grasses.

related low-water plants: Opium or breadseed poppy (*Papaver somniferum*), with pale blue-green foliage and large flowers in red, pink, lilac, white, or maroon-black, is often double-flowered. 'Lauren's Grape', selected by the author, is a single-flowered, grape purple seed strain.

Phacelia campanularia

desert bluebell

grows 6–12 inches tall and 3–6 inches wide

best in all zones, cool-season annual, resents humid heat

special attributes: A small southwestern native with cobalt blue flowers and sparse hairy maroon-tinted foliage, desert bluebell blooms for a few weeks and then disappears soon thereafter. Beloved of bees and bumblebees. Self-sows some. Like many other plants in the *Phacelia* genus, may cause an itchy rash upon touching in sensitive individuals.

design ideas: Stunning with California poppies. Consorts comfortably with smaller cacti. Sow in sheets between yuccas and agaves for a seasonal carpet of rich color or intermingle with smaller perennials and annuals such as golden fleece, four-nerve daisy, blackfoot daisy, sundrops, and sulfur flower.

related low-water plants: *Phacelia sericea* is a slightly larger, very hardy, short-lived perennial with silvery leaves and lavender flowers. *Phacelia congesta, P. tanacetifolia, P. viscida,* and *P. parryi* are all lavender-blue annuals, as are the closely related baby blue eyes, *Nemophila menziesii* and *N. phacelioides*.

Thymophylla tenuiloba (formerly *Dyssodia tenuiloba*)

golden fleece, Dahlberg daisy

grows 6–12 inches tall and 10–15 inches wide

best in all zones, warm-season annual, short-lived perennial in frost-free regions

special attributes: This southwestern native forms tidy, diminutive mounds of ferny, light green, citrus-scented leaves that provide a lush backdrop for clouds of tiny yellow daisies late spring to frost, attractive to butterflies and bees. Self-sows mildly. Feeds caterpillars of the dainty sulfur butterfly.

design ideas: Use as edging or foreground plant along sidewalks Plant in rock gardens as soft-textured contrast to boulders, smaller yuccas, agaves, and cacti. Combine with California poppy, desert bluebell, blackfoot daisy, and hummingbird trumpet.

related low-water plants: Southwestern native *parralena* (*Thymophylla pentachaeta*) is a dwarf subshrub with similar flowers and foliage hardy in zones 8–10.

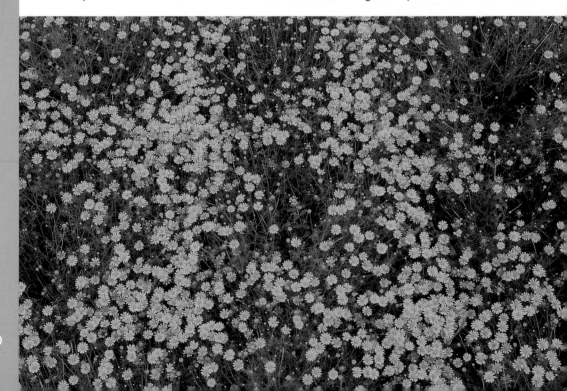

Viola corsica

Corsican pansy

grows 4–10 inches tall and wide

best in zones 4–10, short-lived perennial, cool-season annual in extreme climates

special attributes: This tireless bloomer takes a break from its endless parade of large, deep purple flowers during the heat of the summer or may sometimes succumb at this point and return in the fall from volunteer seedlings. Peak bloom is spring in cold climates, and fall and winter in milder ones. In snowless winters, often blooms on sunny days despite cold temperatures, swarmed by grateful bees. Self-sows with abandon. Flowers very rarely creamy white. Feeds caterpillars of several fritillary butterflies.

design ideas: Lovely early in the season with cushion phlox, dwarf bearded iris, and species tulips, or under deciduous trees with grape hyacinth and Grecian windflower. In mild regions, interplant amid autumn daffodils for a gold and purple fall display, and with creamy white 'Grand Primo' narcissus for winter.

Succulents and Cacti

These architectural plants store water in stems and leaves
sometimes defended by sharp spines. They are dependable
performers in dry gardens, with a quirky beauty year-round,
often offering stunningly beautiful flowers as well. In cold
regions, hardy cacti and succulents naturally shrivel in winter to
help endure subfreezing temperatures; plants reabsorb moisture
and plump up in spring. All prefer fast-draining soils low in
organic matter. Padded cacti and succulents that make offsets are
easy to propagate.

Aloe maculata hybrid (formerly *Aloe saponaria*)

spotted aloe, soap aloe

grows 12–18 inches tall and wide, makes offsets

best in zones 8b–10

special attributes: The spotted leaves of this heirloom aloe are edged in sharp teeth and make broad clustering rosettes. Branched stems up to 3 feet tall with heads of coral orange flowers make a show from late winter to spring and repeat intermittently year-round, attracting hummingbirds and bees. Tips of leaves turn purple and partially die back in hard frost, renewing in spring. Thrives in coastal conditions.

design ideas: Use as a flowering evergreen accent for narrow strips near paving. Combine with blue tree yucca, spineless prickly pear, feather grass, silver spurge, and golden fleece. Roof garden plant.

related low-water succulents: Some of the hardier aloes include *Aloe grandidentata* and hybrids of *A. maculata* with *A. striata* and *A. vera*, all spring-flowering heirlooms that offset prolifically. The hardiest, *A. aristata*, makes clusters of dwarf rosettes with pointed dark green leaves flecked white, is hardy to zone 6 in the West.

Bulbine frutescens

cat's tail

grows 10–18 inches tall and 18–30 inches wide

best in zones 8–10

special attributes:
Grassy succulent leaves give cat's tail a lush look. Spikes of small star-shaped yellow or orange flowers with feathery gold stamens flush fall through spring and sporadically on through summer, attracting bees. Propagates easily from cuttings taken near the base of the stem. Juice from leaves has healing properties like *Aloe vera*. 'Tiny Tangerine' (pictured) is a compact selection.

design ideas: Makes a flowering evergreen accent ideal for narrow strips near paving. Combine with blue barrel cactus, agave, feather grass, silver spurge, and rosemary. Roof garden plant.

related low-water succulents: *Bulbine narcissifolia* makes clumps of twisting gray leaves. *Bulbine abyssinica* forms bushy tufts of green leaves. Both have rounded heads of golden flowers, grow less than 1 foot tall, and are hardy in zones 6–10.

Cylindropuntia whipplei 'Snow Leopard' (formerly *Opuntia whipplei*)

'Snow Leopard' cholla

grows 3–5 feet tall and wide

best in zones 5–10 with low humidity

special attributes: This distinctive shrubby southwestern cactus is covered in dense, glistening white spines. Pale yellow flowers appear at the tips of stems in summer. Among the larger hardy cacti. Spiny branches and fruits detach readily, can be hazardous; locate away from paths.

design ideas: Silhouette against dark green conifers or near a masonry wall. Plant as a specimen where sun backlights the showy spines. Combine with other cacti, agaves, yuccas, sotols, grasses, desert four o'clock, datura, cloud daisy, penstemons.

related low-water cacti: Thistle cholla (*Cylindropuntia davisii*), with golden spines and green or black flowers, makes a formidable 3- to 4-foot shrub. Tree cholla (*C. imbricata*) makes an upright shrub to 6 feet or more with tiers of succulent branches armed with vicious spines, adapts to humid climates. Large magenta flowers appear on upper branches in summer, attracting bees. Fruits ripen yellow in fall.

Echinocereus coccineus

claret cup, hedgehog cactus

grows 6–24 inches tall, makes many stems, forming clusters to 3 feet wide

best in zones 5–10

special attributes: Claret cup is a southwestern native cactus with barrel-shaped or columnar ribbed stems armed with slender spines. Clusters make attractive, bold clumps. Long-lasting scarlet flowers open in spring, attracting hummingbirds. Female plants ripen reddish edible fruits.

design ideas: Plant in between stones in rock gardens; combine with smaller yuccas and agaves, pale stonecrop, ice plants, mountain basket of gold.

related low-water cacti: *Echinocereus triglochidiatus* is a closely related claret cup; a spineless mounding form is var. *mojavensis* f. *inermis*; 'White Sands' is a robust spiny selection to 2 feet tall. *Echinocereus ×roetteri* (formerly *E. lloydii*) is a natural hybrid with pink to orange flowers. *Echinocereus reichenbachii*, *E. albispinus*, and *E. baileyi* are small, slowly clustering species with lacy spines, rosy purple flowers. All are hardy to zone 5.

Euphorbia rigida (formerly *Euphorbia biglandulosa*)

silver spurge

grows 1–2 feet tall and 2–3 feet wide

best in zones 6–10, deciduous in zone 5 in the West

special attributes: The thick stems of silver spurge are covered in overlapping pointed gray-blue leaves topped late winter or early spring with small clustered flowers surrounded by greenish yellow bracts, attracting bees. Foliage sometimes tinges bronze or red in cold weather. Stems and leaves exude irritating milky latex if bruised.

design ideas: This spurge's unusual texture and early color looks good with almost anything. Use as a sculptural accent for narrow strips near paving or to give needed contrast amid succulents, agaves and yuccas, and subshrubs such as silver germander, artemisia, lavender, rosemary, ceniza, and Jerusalem sage. Good roof garden plant.

related low-water succulents: Morocco mound (*Euphorbia resinifera*), zones 8b–10 with low humidity, makes gray to sage green 2- to 3-foot mounds of four-sided succulent stems with short paired spines.

Ferocactus glaucescens

blue barrel

grows 1–2 feet tall and wide, makes offsets

best in zones 8b–10

special attributes: This robust globular Mexican cactus is edged with rows of golden spines along bluish ribs. Rings of yellow flowers appear around the top of the plant in spring, attracting bees. A form that is spineless or nearly so is *Ferocactus glaucescens* f. *nuda* (*inermis*), with slightly smaller, straw-toned flowers. More humidity tolerant than most barrel cacti.

design ideas: Create a modern look with pale stonecrop and small agaves. Plant between stones in rock gardens. Combine with perky Sue, golden fleece, desert bluebell, verbena.

related low-water cacti: Golden barrel (*Echinocactus grusonii*), with dense golden spines, is as hardy as blue barrel but does not adapt as well to high humidity. Southwestern native horse crippler, *E. texensis* (zones 6–10), makes low spiny domes to 1 foot wide, has large pinkish orange flowers and showy edible red fruits.

Graptopetalum paraguayense

ghost plant

grows 6 inches tall and 24–36 inches wide

best in zones 7b–10

special attributes:
This Mexican succulent makes branching pendant stems carrying rosettes of lavender-tinged gray-blue leaves in dense masses. Delicate maroon-spotted starlike flowers appear occasionally but offer minor interest. Propagates readily from stem cuttings or leaves. Leaves detach easily; protect from traffic. Avoid positions in hot sun.

design ideas: Use in raised planters, between stones in rock gardens and masonry walls, in troughs and roof gardens. Combine with silver ponyfoot and giant prairie lily.

related low-water succulents: ×*Graptosedum* 'Francesco Baldi' has narrow pink-tinged gray-green leaves, performs better in strong sun. One of its parents, blue *Sedum pachyphyllum*, has smaller leaves and rosettes. *Sedum palmeri* and *S. confusum* prefer part shade. They make draping branches with rosettes of flattened pale green leaves and have showy yellow flowers in late winter. All are hardy to zone 8.

Opuntia aurea 'Coombe's Winter Glow'

'Coombe's Winter Glow' beavertail cactus

grows 1 foot tall and 5 feet wide

best in zones 5–8, also zones 9–10 in the West, resents humidity

special attributes: A hardy western native, beavertail cactus grows in sprawling mounds of thick flattened pads that turn showy purple tones in winter cold; large rose pink flowers appear in early summer, attracting bees. Stems lack true spines but carry tufts of tiny barbed glochids that, though less fiercely painful, can be irritating for some time.

design ideas: Combine with silver spurge, yucca, grasses, artemisia, ice plants, pale stonecrop, buckwheats.

related low-water cacti: Black-spined prickly pear (*Opuntia macrocentra*) forms robust shrubs, has red-centered yellow flowers and lavender-tinted pads that turn purple in cold or drought. *Opuntia chlorotica* var. *santa-rita* is larger and even more purple. Both are hardy to zone 7. *Opuntia polyacantha* makes white-spined, creeping mounds with yellow to rose red flowers, is hardy to zone 4; 'Dark Knight' and 'Purple Desert' are selections with rosy flowers and showy purple winter pads.

Opuntia cacanapa 'Ellisiana'

spineless prickly pear

grows 4–5 feet tall and wide

best in zones 7–10

special attributes: This spineless heirloom selection of a shrubby southwestern native prickly pear has oval gray-green pads bearing large yellow flowers in early summer; these attract bees. Maroon fruits ripen in fall, persist through winter. Tolerates humidity as well as desert conditions.

design ideas: Use as an informal hedge or silhouette as a specimen near a wall. Mingle with grasses, aromatic aster, ceniza, rosemary, silver germander, agave, sotol, and yucca.

related low-water cacti: Tulip prickly pear (*Opuntia phaeacantha*) has flattened pads edged with brown-tipped spines. Large flowers may be yellow with red centers, or shades of pink, peach, or orange, depending on the cultivar. Fleshy plum-colored fruits last through early winter. Eastern native *O. humifusa* 'Inermis' makes sprawling mats of spineless green pads with yellow flowers in spring, red fruit in fall; tolerates humidity. Both are hardy in zones 5–8.

Sempervivum tectorum

houseleek, hens and chicks

grows 2 inches tall and 2–6 inches wide, makes offsets

best in zones 4–7, also zones 8–10 on the West Coast, resents humid heat

special attributes: This heirloom makes dense rosettes of fleshy pale green leaves with tips tinged bronze. Mature rosettes send up downy 1-foot stalks of starry reddish flowers in early summer, attracting bees. Rosettes die after bloom and are replaced by young offsets.

design ideas: Nest between stones in rock gardens, troughs, masonry walls, in roof gardens. Plant in narrow strips near paving.

related low-water succulents: Cobweb houseleek (*Sempervivum arachnoideum*) makes small globular rosettes covered in white down. *Sempervivum calcareum* makes flattened green rosettes tipped burgundy. *Echeveria runyonii* (zones 8–10) has scalloped gray rosettes and showy bright orange flowers in nodding spikes in summer, attracting hummingbirds. It is the most humidity tolerant of the beautiful and varied *Echeveria* clan, which typically does best in zones 9–10 on the West Coast.

Palms and Cycads

Although palms and cycads are commonly associated with the lush tropics, those included here actually tolerate drought and hard frost. Prolonged or severe cold can damage foliage in unusually harsh years, but new leaves sprout quickly to replace the lost canopy. Palms and cycads establish best when soil temperatures are warm.

Brahea armata (formerly *Erythea armata*)

Mexican blue palm

grows slowly to 30 feet tall or more with 8- to 10-foot-wide crown

best in zones 8b–10 in the West

special attributes: This stately Mexican palm has a thick solitary trunk and fan-shaped powder blue fronds on stiff, thorny stems. Big creamy flower spikes arch from the crown, attracting bees, and later ripen grapelike clusters of fruit. Natural thatching of old foliage offers nesting for birds; if a tidier look is desired, it can be removed. Trees with trunks less than 3 feet tall transplant best from containers.

design ideas: Use as a specimen tree. Combine with the lacy textures of artemisia, bird of paradise shrub, and desert willow, or with the bold forms of larger agaves, sotols, and prickly pears.

related low-water palms: *Brahea clara* is slightly less blue, more humidity tolerant; *B. moorei* also tolerates humidity, makes a shade-loving dwarf with green fronds powdered silver beneath. Desert fan palm (*Washingtonia filifera*) is a tall, fast-growing southwestern native with massive trunks and gray-green leaves held on thorny stems.

Chamaedorea radicalis

hardy feather palm

grows slowly to 3–6 feet tall (to 10 feet in trunking forms) and 3–4 feet wide

best in zones 8b–10

special attributes: This dwarf Mexican palm makes fountains of arching feathery fronds that create an exotic, lush appearance belying its hardiness. Short solitary stems carry foliage that remains dark shining green all year. Females bear stalks with hollylike clusters of red fruit ripening throughout the year. Trunking strains such as 'Soledad' slowly develop tall bamboolike stems to 10 feet.

design ideas: Graceful foliage for understory plantings. Assumes different looks as sunlight strikes at varied angles during the day; place where plants can be viewed from interior windows. Plant in groups for full effect and to assure pollination for pretty fruit.

related low-water palms: Hardy bamboo palm (*Chamaedorea microspadix*) forms clustering stems to 10 feet with coarsely divided apple green foliage, grayish beneath. Red fruit on female plants.

Chamaerops humilis var. *cerifera*

Atlas mountain palm

grows 8–12 feet tall and wide

best in zones 8–10

special attributes:
A shrubby palm with fan-shaped silvery blue leaves on spiny stalks, Atlas mountain palm branches to make a dense mounding specimen. Clusters of small creamy yellow flowers appear on male plants in late winter; female blossoms are inconspicuous and ripen russet leathery grapelike fruits in summer. New stems form at base of trunk; if desired, remove to create tree form. Thrives in coastal conditions.

design ideas: Plant as a specimen or in groups; good for informal hedges. Combine with succulents and grasses. Shimmering foliage nice for evening gardens.

related low-water palms: Mediterranean fan palm (*Chamaerops humilis* var. *humilis*) has olive green foliage, grows slightly larger to 15 feet tall and wide. Mazari palm (*Nannorrhops ritchiana*) is slow growing but equally large with branching stems and gray-green to silvery foliage, thrives in desert heat.

Cycas revoluta

sago palm

grows 4 feet tall and wide, eventually to 6 feet tall and wide or more

best in zones 8b–10

special attributes: The palmlike waxy dark green fronds of this popular cycad create symmetrical crowns atop shaggy brown water-storing trunks; offsets form multiple heads. Sets of new leaves appear annually. Some years, male or female cones form on mature plants instead of leaves. Thrives in coastal conditions.

design ideas: Interesting on slopes; adapts to difficult dry shade as well as sun. Plant in groups or as a specimen. Combine with trailing lantana, purple heart, and other colorful ground covers. Makes a stunning dark backdrop to tazetta daffodils.

related low-water cycads: *Cycas panzhihuaensis* has a softer, looser habit and dark green to blue-green leaves, flushes new growth more than once a year.

Dioon angustifolium (formerly *Dioon edule* var. *angustifolium*)

virgin palm, *chamal*

grows 3–4 feet wide, eventually solitary or clumping to 6 feet tall and wide

best in zones 8b–10

special attributes: This lush-looking Mexican native, attractive all year, has stiff, spine-tipped fronds forming open rosettes around bulbous stems. New sets of leaves emerge pink to tan all at once in summer, mature blue-green. Distinctive cones appear on separate male and female plants in alternate years. Give part shade in desert heat.

design ideas: Interesting on slopes and in roof gardens. Adapts to dry shade as well as sun. Plant as a specimen near a masonry wall. Combine with agaves, grasses, blue sedge, velvet creeper, spineless prickly pear, silver spurge, and California poppy.

related low-water cycads: *Dioon edule* 'Queretaro' produces upright foliage, emerges powder blue, performs well in hot sun.

220

Phoenix canariensis

Canary Island date palm

grows 30–40 feet tall or more with 25- to 40-foot-wide crown

best in zones 8b–10

special attributes: This majestic palm carries rich green, leafy crowns with up to 100 gracefully arching featherlike fronds; sharp spines near the base of leaves command respect. Massive tan trunks are embossed with diamond patterns. Cut off old leaves to retain short stem bases, or trim more closely to develop pineapple-like effect. Small flowers on branched yellowish stems appear in winter, attracting bees. Female trees ripen clusters of bright orange fruits in fall. Phytoplasma diseases limit use in a few areas.

design ideas: Use as a shade or specimen tree where space allows; beautiful at all stages of growth. Good in groups for avenues or allees.

related low-water palms: True date palm (*Phoenix dactylifera*) has blue-gray foliage and suckering stems, happiest in low humidity. Sugar date palm (*Phoenix sylvestris*) and pindo palm (*Butia odorata*, formerly known as *B. capitata*) are intermediate-size feather-leafed palms with gray-green foliage, better for hot, humid regions than *P. canariensis*.

Rhapidophyllum hystrix

needle palm

grows 6–10 feet tall and wide

best in zones 6b–10

special attributes: This remarkably hardy shrub palm, native to the Southeast, forms clumps of fan-shaped deep green leaves, pale beneath. Short hairy stems slowly increase by suckers, bear scattered black needlelike spines. Female plants ripen small clusters of grapelike seeds. Add lime for best growth on very acid soils.

design ideas: Dark green and silver-backed foliage plays with light and shadow. Plant as a specimen or in groups in the open or in woodland understory. Combine with grasses and crinums. Good choice for informal hedge, as specimen near foundation or walkway, or in large outdoor container.

related low-water palms: *Guihaia argyrata* has green fronds felted silver beneath. Southeastern native saw palmetto (*Serenoa repens*) makes branched creeping stems with bright green to silvery blue fans on spiny stalks; flowers are night-fragrant; both are hardy in zones 8b–10.

Zamia integrifolia

coontie

grows 36–48 inches wide and 18–24 inches tall

best in zones 8b–10

special attributes: This dwarf cycad native to Florida and Georgia grows from fleshy underground stems. Heads of fernlike rich green leaves give a lush appearance all year. Fronds do not scratch like other cycads and may be wide and dense or narrow and lacy; new leaves unfurl annually in summer. Male and female cones appear on separate plants in spring. Fleshy red fruits mature in fall.

design ideas: Adapts to difficult dry shade as well as sun. Plant as a specimen, in groupings, or on edges near paving. Combine with tazetta daffodil, velvet creeper, oxblood lily. Roof garden plant.

related low-water cycads: Mexican *Ceratozamia kuesteriana* makes graceful 4- to 5-foot-wide rosettes of feathery olive green fronds, clusters slowly; new leaves emerge brown. *Ceratozamia latifolia* has bolder texture, with coppery new foliage emerging midsummer.

Fiber Plants

Plants in this group make dramatic rosettes of tough, fiber-filled leaves sometimes harvested to make rope. They bring strong architectural lines to gardens. In cold winter climates, fiber plants enjoy positions with full sun; in hot regions they also grow well in filtered shade, where they need even less water to thrive. Yuccas and agaves often look very different as seedlings from their mature appearance, so be aware that the character of the plant may change as it grows.

Aechmea recurvata

hardy bromeliad

grows 6–12 inches tall and 4–8 inches wide, makes offsets

best in zones 8b–10

special attributes: Urn-shaped rosettes of leathery pointed leaves capture and store rainwater, and provide favored habitat for small lizards and toads. Mature plants produce conelike rose-, red-, purple-, or orange-tinted bracts around small pink to blue flowers in fall, winter, or spring, attracting hummingbirds. Rosettes wither after bloom and are replaced by offsets.

design ideas: Ideal for thin soil near the base of trees and for roof gardens. Nest between or on stones or as an epiphyte on trees.

related low-water bromeliads: Matchstick bromeliad, *Aechmea gamosepala*, makes bright green rosettes with blunt-tipped foliage and in late winter sends up showy blue flowers on long-lasting reddish stalks. *Dyckia fosteriana* and *D. platyphylla* form spiny silver, maroon, or bronze clustering rosettes with branched stalks of orange flowers in spring. *Puya venusta* makes silvery rosettes with spikes of turquoise flowers in winter on rosy pink stems.

Agave gentryi (formerly *Agave macroculmis*)

green century plant

grows 4 feet tall and 6 feet wide, makes offsets

best in zones 7b–10

special attributes: The leaves of this large green century plant often show decorative gray highlights and spine imprinting and are armed with curved spines on the margins. Rosettes mature in 7 to 10 years and send up massive 12-foot stalks in late winter with tiered clusters of golden flowers; the rosettes die after flowering, leaving offsets to carry on. Bees, sphinx moths, hummingbirds, and bats adore the flowers. 'Jaws' is a selection with undulating, extra spiny leaves.

design ideas: Plant as an accent or group near masonry walls. Combine in sun with ceniza, trailing lantana, perky Sue, Texas betony, feather grass, and autumn embers muhly. In part shade combine with oxblood lily, ghost plant, velvet creeper, Palmer's sedum.

related low-water agaves: Similar green *Agave salmiana* 'Ferox' offsets prolifically. Texan and Mexican natives *A. asperrima* (formerly *A. scabra*) and *A. americana* subsp. *protoamericana* have rougher, straight or sinuous gray to pale green foliage, create numerous hybrids; most tolerate humidity and shade as well as considerable cold.

Agave havardiana

Big Bend century plant

grows 2 feet tall and 3–4 feet wide, solitary or offsetting

best in zones 6–10

special attributes: This Texan century plant has stiff, wide gray leaves edged in black spines. Rosettes mature in 7 to 10 years and send up 10-foot summer stalks with tiered clusters of golden flowers attractive to bees, hummingbirds, sphinx moths, and bats; the rosettes die after flowering, but sometimes leave offsets.

design ideas: Plant as a specimen or cluster to silhouette against masonry walls. Combine with ice plants, buckwheats, and hummingbird trumpet; with sculptural cacti, blue joint fir, and New Mexican olive; or with soft-textured feather grass, autumn embers muhly, and Apache plume.

related low-water agaves: Whale's tongue (*Agave ovatifolia*), zones 7b–10, makes spectacular solitary rosettes to 5 feet tall and 6 feet wide with broad, distinctively cupped blue-gray leaves edged with black to gray spines.

Agave parryi

hardy century plant

grows 12–18 inches tall and 18–30 inches wide, makes offsets

best in zones 6–10, worth trying in zone 5b in the West

special attributes: This compact southwestern native century plant makes prolific rosettes of stiff gray leaves edged in black spines. Rosettes

mature in 7 to 10 years, then send up 10-foot stalks in summer with tiered clusters of golden flowers attractive to bees, hummingbirds, sphinx moths, and bats; the rosettes die and are replaced by many offsets.

design ideas: Plant on slopes, in roof gardens. Combine with crocus, *Tulipa batalinii*, California poppy, desert bluebell, pussytoes, ice plants, buckwheats, smaller cacti.

related low-water agaves: *Agave parryi* var. *neomexicana* produces suckering rosettes with many narrow leaves tipped with long black spines, flowers in spring. 'Sunspot' is a variegated form. *Agave parryi* var. *truncata* 'Huntington' is a compact, artichoke-like, clumping blue-gray selection, not as hardy.

Agave striata

narrow-leaf century plant

grows 12–18 inches tall and 18–36 inches wide

best in zones 7b–10

special attributes: This century plant has rosettes with narrow, wickedly pointed pale gray-green to bluish leaves that can be stiff or curving and that may take on pretty purple tones in cold or drought. Mature rosettes send up unbranched 6-foot flower spikes and create new rosettes by division after flowering. Position away from paths or trim spines to avoid injury.

design ideas: Plant on slopes or in roof gardens, in crevices of vertical walls. Combine in sun with Texas betony, giant prairie lily, wine cup, silver ponyfoot; in part shade with ghost plant, oxblood lilies, velvet creeper, Palmer's sedum.

related low-water agaves: Squid agave (*Agave bracteosa*) makes pale green rosettes of spineless, undulating, narrow, flexible leaves, increases by offsets. *Agave mitis* (formerly *A. celsii*) makes open rosettes of broad glossy green or pale blue leaves edged with harmless soft spines, divides slowly to make clumps. Both prefer part shade, are hardy in zones 8–10.

Agave victoriae-reginae

Queen Victoria's century plant

grows 12–15 inches tall and wide

best in zones 8–10

special attributes: Queen Victoria's century plant has globular rosettes of many short angular leaves with white margins. Young plants sometimes produce offsets, while larger rosettes often remain solitary. After 10 to 12 years, plants send up unbranched 6-foot flower spikes. Several compact selections and variegated forms exist.

design ideas: Group in rock gardens as accents. Plant on slopes and in roof gardens, in crevices of vertical walls. Combine in sun with cacti, in part shade with ghost plant, velvet creeper, and Palmer's sedum.

related low-water agaves: *Agave ferdinandi-regis*, with larger white-edged leaves, and 'Sharkskin', with artichoke-like dark gray rosettes, are probable hybrids with *A. asperrima*. Compact selections of *A. lophantha*, zones 7b–10, make green rosettes with prominent marginal spines and pale stripes down the center of the leaves, multiply steadily. 'Quadricolor' is a striking variegated form.

Dasylirion wheeleri

blue sotol

grows 4–6 feet tall and wide

best in zones 6–10 with low humidity

special attributes: This southwestern native has rosettes of flexible blue-gray leaves edged in golden spines and tipped with white fibers. Male plants send up tawny gold spikes in spring; females hoist greenish plumes ripening straw-colored seeds. Bees relish the flowers. Mature plants divide to form multiheaded clumps.

design ideas: Plant near masonry walls for shadow effects, or on slopes. Combine with ceniza, anise hyssop, penstemons, cacti, feather grass, or buffalograss. Position where sun backlights the striking form and yellow spines.

related low-water sotols: Texas sotol (*Dasylirion texanum*) has more compact olive green foliage. Less hardy *D. berlandieri*, to zone 8, has silvery blue leaves, tolerates some shade where it develops a more relaxed form. Both are better in humid climates than blue sotol. Mexican grass tree (*D. quadrangulatum*, formerly *D. longissimum*) has many cordlike gray-green leaves and a trunk that grows to 6 feet tall; hardy in zones 8–10. Beargrasses *Nolina microcarpa* and *N. texana* form loose, arching clumps of wiry olive green foliage, hardy in zones 5b–10.

Hesperaloe parviflora

red yucca

grows 2–3 feet tall and wide, makes offsets

best in zones 5b–10 with hot summers

special attributes: This yuccalike Texas native has spineless, arching, pliant leaves edged in white filaments. Slender branched stalks bearing bell-shaped coral red or yellow flowers appear in spring and bloom all summer, are favored by hummingbirds and bees. Foliage turns purple in cold weather and drought.

design ideas: Plant as an accent or group near masonry walls, in narrow beds near paving. Good for roof gardens. Combine with silver ceniza, autumn sage, rosemary, santolina, and cacti. Interplant velvet creeper, feather grass, autumn embers muhly, and ice plants. Place where sun backlights the glowing flowers and striking form.

related low-water plants: *Hesperaloe campanulata* has narrow foliage and tall flower spikes with glistening pink flowers. *Hesperaloe funifera* bears stiffly erect olive green leaves and spikes with white flowers. Both are hardy in zones 8–10 and have nocturnal flowers visited by sphinx moths and bats.

233

Yucca baccata

banana yucca

grows 3–4 feet tall and wide, makes clusters

best in zones 5b–10 with low humidity

special attributes: Banana yucca is a southwestern native with broad, stiff, spine-tipped olive green to blue-gray leaves edged in white fibers that catch light, frost, and snowflakes. Boldest of the cold-hardy yuccas. Fat spikes of creamy white flowers, often tinged pink, appear in early summer and ripen fleshy fruits.

design ideas: Plant as an accent or group near masonry walls. Combine with ice plants, evening primrose, penstemons, scarlet betony, and buckwheats, or rabbitbrush, threadleaf sage, New Mexican olive, Apache plume, blue joint fir, and cacti.

related low-water yuccas: Southwestern giant dagger (*Yucca faxoniana*), zones 6–10, has a thick solitary trunk to 10 feet with stiff green leaves and massive clusters of flowers. *Yucca treculeana* has a more slender, branching trunk and flowers in late winter. Southeastern Spanish dagger (*Y. aloifolia*) makes spreading clumps, flowers in early summer, tolerates shade and humidity; several variegated forms are available. Both hardy in zones 7–10.

Yucca elata (formerly *Yucca radiosa*)

soaptree yucca

grows 6–10 feet tall, with 3- to 4-foot-wide heads of foliage

best in zones 5–10 with low humidity

special attributes: This shaggy-stemmed southwestern native carries heads of slender olive green leaves edged in silvery filaments. Bell-shaped greenish white flowers appear in clusters on tall slender stalks in summer. Trunks may remain solitary or branch sparingly. Select forms are especially hairy and have more foliage. Has a taproot, so transplant from containers only. Most reliable trunking yucca for cold climates.

design ideas: Plant near masonry walls or with backdrop of dark green conifers. Combine with pussytoes, ice plants, wine cup, evening primrose, buckwheats, verbena, penstemon, cactus.

Plant where sun backlights hairy foliage and highlights distinctive form.

related low-water yuccas: Similarly hairy olive green *Yucca constricta* of south-central Texas makes clusters of stemless rosettes or may have short trunks to 3 feet. Great Plains yucca (*Y. glauca*), zones 4–8, carries looser clustered heads, unbranched spikes of flowers in early summer. Both are more tolerant of humidity.

Yucca filamentosa

Adam's needle

grows 2–3 feet tall and wide, forms clusters

best in zones 5–9

special attributes: This yucca is a southeastern native with flexible leaves edged in white filaments. Clustering relaxed rosettes that look lusher and less threatening than other yuccas send up branched spikes of showy white flowers. Thrives in coastal conditions and humidity but not in hot desert conditions. Variegated selections include 'Golden Sword', 'Color Guard' (pictured), and 'Bright Edge'.

design ideas: Plant in groups or as a specimen. Combine with wine cup, verbena, scarlet betony, evening primrose, sedge. Place variegated selections to catch backlighting from sun.

related low-water yuccas: Also native to the Southeast, *Yucca recurvifolia*, zones 7–10, makes leafy, drooping rosettes that cluster and sometimes branch with trunks to 6 feet. Flowers appear in spring, summer, or fall. 'Glauca' has blue-green foliage; 'Margaritaville' and 'Gold Ribbons' are variegated. Southeastern native *Yucca gloriosa* makes stiffer rosettes, also with several variegated forms.

Yucca harrimaniae

dollhouse yucca

grows 6–12 inches tall and wide, makes clusters

best in zones 4–8, resents humid heat

special attributes: This is an especially cute yucca from the interior West, making a sunburst of gray-green foliage edged in pale hairlike, often profuse and curly filaments. Spikes of large bell-shaped creamy flowers appear some years in early summer.

design ideas: Makes an excellent companion to small cacti. Plant into a carpet of ice plants or pussytoes. Combine with lavenderleaf sundrop, blackfoot daisy, four-nerve daisy, plains skullcap, scarlet betony, verbena, and pineleaf penstemon.

related low-water yuccas: *Yucca nana* is on the smaller end of the more variable size range of *Y. harrimaniae*. Its foliage is wider, sometimes strikingly blue, and typically sparser in the rosette. Some selections of *Y. neomexicana* are so similar to *Y. nana* as to be almost indistinguishable.

Yucca pallida

pale-leaf yucca

grows 1–2 feet tall and wide, makes offsets

best in zones 6–10

special attributes: This humidity tolerant Texas native grows from slowly creeping rootstocks and makes rosettes of wide, pliant, flattened or twisted gray-green to silvery blue leaves. Translucent yellow margins catch light and deserve respect for small but sharp serrations. Slender 3- to 5-foot stalks of white flowers appear late spring to summer.

design ideas: Combine in sun with ceniza, trailing lantana, perky Sue, Texas betony, Mexican feather grass, and autumn embers muhly; or in part shade with oxblood lilies, ghost plant, velvet creeper, and Palmer's sedum. Plant where sun backlights foliage to highlight golden edges and distinctive form. Roof garden plant.

related low-water yuccas: Twist leaf yucca (*Yucca rupicola*) of south-central Texas is an olive green version of pale-leaf yucca. Nodding yucca (*Y. cernua*) from southeastern Texas makes handsome bluish rosettes with loose spikes of pendant flowers. Both tolerate humidity.

Yucca rostrata

blue tree yucca

grows 6–15 feet tall with 2- to 3-foot-wide heads of foliage

best in zones 7–10, worth trying in zone 6 in the west

special attributes: This is a palmlike southwestern yucca with one to several heads of slender, flexible gray-blue leaves on shaggy branches. Large clusters of pendant white flowers appear on 3- to 5-foot stems in late spring. Thatch can be trimmed to expose trunks. Tolerates both desert and more humid conditions.

design ideas: Plant as a specimen for desert gardens. Combine with bird of paradise shrub, desert willow, datura, agave, bull muhly, giant sacaton, large prickly pears. Mingle with larger grasses. Pale, pliant foliage shimmers and rustles in evening gardens.

related low-water yuccas: Similar *Yucca thompsoniana*, zones 6–10, has stiffer, shorter, blue or olive green leaves with sharp golden edges, makes shrubby or treelike specimens with several heads and showy flowers. *Yucca linearifolia*, zones 7–10, has extremely narrow, flexible gray-blue or green leaves and shaggy trunks with few or no branches. Creamy flowers are in compact, short-stemmed clusters. Both perform equally well in desert or more humid climates.

Index

Page numbers in bold type indicate main text sections and pages with photographs.

About the Authors

Lauren Springer Ogden and Scott Ogden's horticultural experience in the United States and Europe spans zones 4 through 10. They design public and private gardens, speak widely, and have written three books each, including their award-winning book *Plant-Driven Design*. They seek plants and design inspiration in the wilds of the United States as well as Mexico, South Africa, and Argentina; several of their plant introductions are in the nursery trade. At home in the challenging climates of Fort Collins, Colorado, and Austin, Texas, they tend two intensive gardens together.